# FLYING HIGH IN THE SKY

## *Letters from a Pan Am Stewardess*

*Marie Louise McGrath*

## Carol Ann Patterson Boyles-Jernigan

Jan-Carol
Publishing, Inc
*"every story needs a book"*

Flying High in the Sky:
Letters from a Pan Am Stewardess
Carol Ann Patterson Boyles-Jernigan

Published September 2024
Heirloom Editions
Imprint of Jan-Carol Publishing, Inc.
All rights reserved
Copyright © 2024 Carol Ann Patterson Boyles-Jernigan
Cover and book design: Tara Sizemore
Cover background image: © Lightfield Studios/Adobe Stock
Old letter background: © LiliGraphie/Adobe Stock

ISBN: 978-1-962561-40-2
Library of Congress Control Number: 2024945898

Jan-Carol Publishing, Inc.
PO Box 701
Johnson City, TN 37605
publisher@jancarolpublishing.com
www.jancarolpublishing.com

My book is dedicated to the memory of Marie McGrath,
a stewardess on Pan American World Airlines, 1953–1957.

It is also dedicated to Marie's parents,
Mr. and Mrs. Robert McGrath,
and to her brothers, Jim and Robert McGrath.

# Foreword

By Gregg Herken

In the fall of 1957, Marie McGrath was my fourth-grade teacher at Sunnybrae Elementary School in San Mateo, California. When Marie wasn't flying as a stewardess for Pan Am, she was a substitute teacher at a number of schools in the Bay Area. Since our regular teacher was sick a lot, we often had "Miss McGrath"—as we knew her—in our classroom. We students loved her.

I particularly remember the "luau" that she treated our class to after we had done well on a test, with food that she brought back from Hawaii on the Pan Am Clipper. The "roast pig" was probably Spam, but the pineapple and other fruits were fresh. And I still don't understand why anybody would eat *poi*, which tasted to me like library paste. While we ate, Marie told us stories about her travels to the Islands and around the world. For 10-year-olds, it was very exotic stuff.

In my case, I also had a personal reason for being grateful to Marie. Our family had just moved from Denver to San Mateo, and I was having a difficult time fitting in. Back in Colorado, buckskin coats were all the rage for third-grade boys—it was the time of coonskin caps and Davy Crockett on Disney. I was especially proud of my coat, which had fringe on the sleeves. When I arrived at Sunnybrae for the first day of school, however, the other kids looked at me like I had just fallen off the turnip truck. Obviously, buckskin coats were not the rage in the Peninsula suburbs.

I was too embarrassed to tell my parents about being teased at school, but Marie picked up on it. Evidently, she telephoned my parents and told them, in effect, to lose my old coat. In any case, the next time I went to school I was wearing a brand-new, black-and-orange Giants warmup jacket. The team had recently moved to San Francisco. Suddenly, I was not only accepted by my classmates, but popular.

The day that our principal came on the PA system to announce, "Miss McGrath's plane is missing," is another vivid memory of that time. In my imagination, Clipper *Romance of the Skies*, Pan American Flight 7, had simply flown into a cloud and not flown out again. It was only many years later—when I was working at the Smithsonian's National Air and Space Museum—that I discovered the cause of the crash in mid-Pacific had never been determined.

During my research, however, I also learned that the son of the navigator on the Clipper that fateful day—Ken Fortenberry—was equally involved in the quest to find out what happened to Clipper *Romance*. In April 2023, Ken and I joined with the other members of our Flight 7 Memorial Committee—including those who lost friends or relatives on the Clipper—to dedicate a large granite tablet engraved with the names of the passengers and crew who perished on *Romance of the Skies*. The memorial sits on the grounds of the History Museum at Millbrae City Hall, overlooking San Francisco International Airport, where Marie's Clipper last took flight.

At the dedication ceremony, the pastor of the local Methodist Church read the following passage from Psalm 139:

> *If I rise on wings of morning,*
> *And dwell in the uttermost part of the sea,*
> *Even there thy hand shall lead me,*
> *And thy right hand shall hold me.*

Rest in peace, Miss McGrath. Your students remember and thank you.

# Table of Contents

# Chapter 1

## *The Plane Crash*

I was living in Tallahassee, Florida, employed by Florida State University as a Resident Hall Counselor on the Dean of Women's staff, listening to the radio. As I was leaving my apartment for my office in Reynolds Hall, where I was responsible for 300 freshmen woman students, I heard a news flash that a Pan American Stratocruiser was declared missing in the Pacific Ocean. It was on a flight from San Francisco to Honolulu with a crew of eight and 36 passengers aboard. I was stunned! I was afraid that my dear college friend, Marie McGrath, a stewardess, might be on that plane. I rushed out of Reynolds Hall to purchase the *Tallahassee Democrat*, the local paper, only to discover her picture on the front page with the headline, "Plane, 44 Aboard, Missing Over Pacific."

I was devastated. I could only think of her family and the horror they must be experiencing, not knowing if she would be found alive. I purchased *The Miami Herald* dated Monday, November 10, 1957, with the headline, "Carrier Speeding To Join Massive Hunt for Airliner."

*Carrier Speeding To Join Massive Hunt for Airliner*
*Explosion? U. S. Officials Say: "We Don't Know."*

*A massive search by air and sea was shaping up over the mid-Pacific late Saturday night, in quest of a missing Pan American World Airways Stratocruiser with 44 people aboard. Pacific Fleet headquarters directed the big carrier Philippine Sea to leave Long*

Beach, Calif., at once, hurrying its far-ranging radar-equipped antisubmarine planes into the search. The carrier should reach the area tonight. In San Diego, the Navy ordered two destroyers, the John R. Craig, and the Orleck to depart immediately. Helicopter Squadron 6, near San Diego, was ordered to board the Philippine Sea, as was anti-submarine Squadron 21, a plane unit.

The Pan American Clipper with 36 passengers and 8 crew aboard disappeared Friday without a word that would indicate trouble or disaster. The 5:04 radio call was a routine position report. The pilot didn't make the customary call at 6. The four-engine plane, after passing the "point of no return" halfway, along the 2,400-mile flight to Honolulu, mysteriously vanished without once reporting any trouble. The transport's fuel supply is estimated to have given out at 6 a.m. Miami time. The Coast Guard cutter Minnetonka was part of a search party of more than 29 planes and 14 surface vessels covering a charted checkerboard of 100,000 square miles. The abrupt disappearance of the giant airliner was both baffling and foreboding.

After about a week, the search for Pan Am was ended. All I could think of was Marie and what a tragic end to the life of someone so full of life. She loved being a stewardess, traveling to many foreign cities, and the thrill of meeting many famous celebrities, movie stars, screen writers, and CEOs of movie studios on her flights. I remembered her letters and treasured them all my life. This book reflects Marie's journey, which she narrates through her letters written to me.

# Chapter 2

## *Marie L. McGrath*

Marie Louise McGrath was born in 1931 in Auburn, New York, a city in Cayuga County located at the end of Owasco Lake, one of the Finger Lakes in Central New York State. She was a pretty, energetic, outgoing brunette, enthusiastic about everything she undertook. Her parents were Mr. and Mrs. Robert E. McGrath. She had an older brother, Jim, and a younger brother, Bob.

When she graduated from Auburn High School with her friend, Joyce Lawson, they became roommates at Keuka College, which was, at the time, a women's college located on Keuka Lake in Keuka Park near Penn Yan, New York. During our junior year, Dottie Wingert and I became suitemates with Marie and Joyce in Strong Hall, the cooperative dormitory, which was located about half a mile from the main campus. Each morning, we rode the milk truck to our classes in Hegeman Hall singing, "In My Merry Oldsmobile."

Marie and I both majored in French, and we were active in Terpsichore, the modern dance club. We both loved to dance, and Marie performed arabesques and aerobics in her suite in the morning before classes and in the evening before bedtime.

As a senior, she was elected editor of *Red Jacket*, the college literary magazine, and I joined her as the associate editor. Marie was also a senior class officer and a member of the Honor Society. During the summers, she worked at The Krebs, an "1899 restaurant" located in Skaneateles, NY. Both of us enjoyed many activities together, including four surprise holidays with our classmates.

When Indian Summer arrived, with the hillside's foliage in blazing color, it was tradition for the dean to come to breakfast to declare classes suspended for the day. This was called Surprise Holiday. When this happened, my friends and I would explore the countryside.

One of our favorite places was walking to Garrett Chapel located on Bluff Point overlooking the lake; a memorial to the Garretts' only son, who died of tuberculosis in 1929. We would pick grapes in the vineyards and walk around Esperanza, a beautiful two-and-a-half-story Greek Revival architectural mansion. It was built in 1838 on a bluff overlooking Keuka Lake by a farmer from Virginia, John Nicholas Rose, for his bride. At one time, this property was used as part of the underground railway to harbor slaves leaving the South.

In one of Marie's letters, she reminded me of Surprise Holiday by writing, "Hasn't the weather been beautiful lately? The hillsides look lovely with turning leaves; you should see them from the air. It's simply breathtaking."

Marie's passion throughout college was to become an airline stewardess. Her dream was to fly on Pan Am's Stratocruiser overseas, so she could speak French, which she loved. Under her picture in the college yearbook is written the inscription, "Wanderlust... Air-minded...California."

She got her wish. On the Monday after graduation from Keuka College in 1953, she received a letter from Pan Am inviting her to an interview on June 23, 1953. She was so excited! She splurged some of her graduation money to purchase a ticket to fly to New York City from Syracuse, NY. She wrote me, "There's just no other way to travel once you've flown."

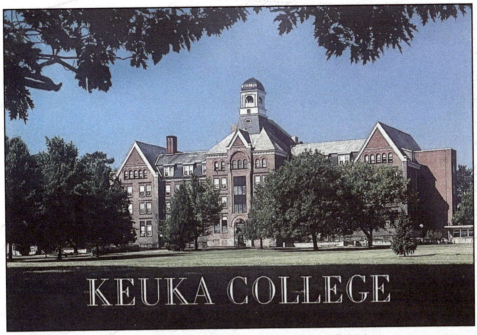

Photo by Bill Banaszewski, Finger Lakes Images Publishers

Keuka Junior Prom
From left to right: Jack, Marie, Carl, Dot, Art, and Carol

Stunt Night
Marie and Carol

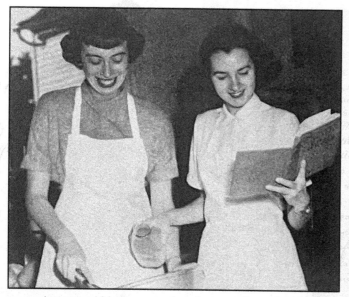

Joyce and Marie preparing dinner at Strong Hall.

Marie and Lili exercising at Strong Hall.

Marie and Carol canoeing on Keuka Lake.

Dot, Carol, Marie, and Joyce during junior year, Strong Hall.

Marie ice skating on Keuka Lake.

The Lawsons and McGraths

Carol, Joyce, and Marie at Marie's home
in Auburn, NY.

Marie, Joyce, Barbara, and Carol at Joyce's home
in Auburn, NY.

Joyce, Marie, Carol, and Dottie at college graduation in 1953.

Carol and Marie at graduation.

Dottie, Carol, and Joyce

Marie, a bridesmaid

Lili and Russell Stepanoff's wedding

Pan American Airways Boeing 377 Stratocruiser (Provided by Terry Morgan)

# Chapter 3

## *Pan American World Airlines*

Marie's wish to become a stewardess came true when she was hired by Pan Am. Her hometown newspaper, *The Citizen-Advertiser*, on Wednesday, February 10, 1954, noted this event with the headline, "Flight Stewardess":

> Miss Marie Louise McGrath, daughter of Mr. and Mrs. Robert McGrath of 60 Capital Street, is now flying with Pan American World Airlines as a flight stewardess. A graduate of Keuka College, Keuka Park, NY, Class of 1953, Miss McGrath will fly to Europe, Africa, and the mid-East in the course of her duties. She serves on clippers, operating out of New York's International Airport to cities as far away as Hong Kong and Johannesburg, South Africa. She flies a maximum of 85 hours per month.

Soon after she began her dream job, she wrote me about her life as a Pan Am Stewardess.

# Chapter 4

## *New York City*
### *June 24, 1953*

arie wrote her letters to me while I was an admissions officer at Keuka College, and when I was a graduate student at the University of Florida. This letter was the first one written to me from New York City when she was interviewed by Pan Am.

*Dear Carol,*

*Just a note from "our town." So much has happened in the few days since graduation! The Monday after, my letter from Pan Am arrived, asking me to be here for an interview on the 23rd! I've been lounging in the sun and reading in the shade — and writing thank you notes in between. Finally found Agnes Turnbull's Gown of Glory in readable print. It's typically Turnbull and makes nice, lazy summer reading.*

*One night, another stewardess and I went to a drive-in and saw Detective Story. That was one of the ten best pictures the year before last and so tense and gripping. It's about a police precinct and tells several stories all at once.*

*Oh yes, Mother bought me a darling dress for her present to the graduate. Remember Stevie's saw-tooth-edged-collar and sleeve dress with the full skirt and green, brown, yellow design? I kept remarking on it. I loved it so, and then when we went to Syracuse Friday to get my ticket, I saw it. And since Stevie* isn't around, who could mind? So, I bought it. There's a crinoline skirt underneath; it puffs way out.

Sunday Betsy and I drove to Cayuga to Brenda's wedding. It was lovely, and there were lots of girls representing Keuka — but such hot weather. Saw Joyce and Rol there — maybe she's written you all this news — hope not — and she says now she has an entirely different job. This one sounds pretty good, too, but I'll believe she'll keep it only when she begins work. Have you heard from Dot? I wonder what she and Bill are doing? Have you heard from Art or any more from Sonny?

Oh, I must tell you about my date. Bob and I play a game of tennis about every day now, and after one of our excursions to the courts, I had to run down street on an errand, and I ran into an old school buddy of mine. He's a graduate of Niagara and has been accepted into Buffalo School of Dentistry. If he does the extra 18 months of graduate work necessary to specialize, he won't have been through his education for six months short of 10 years after high school. Imagine that! Well, we went out Saturday night and had a wonderful time. He used to sit next to me in homeroom, and we had such fun talking and reminiscing. The only thing is — he's the sixth member of our class that I can think of I've dated. He plays the piano beautifully and has received all sorts of scholarships (including full Julliard tuition award) and offers to go on the road. He was something of a child prodigy in music and he told me he used to practice eight hours a day during summer vacations. He's working for a contractor now, and so all day I tried to think of some place where it was nice and not too expensive for dinner. Then he upped and recommended a new ritzy place in Syracuse, followed by a show at 3 Rivers Inn, where the Mills Brothers were starring. We had a tremendous time.

*Carol, in all the confusion of graduation, I left my beanie in the office or on switchboard after you gave it to me. Could you keep it for me until Joyce or I get to Keuka? I wrote the business office asking them to put it away until you arrived. There, I've run out of space and still haven't told you about my trip. Save that 'til next time when I have heard the results of it. Checking out of here — the Allerton Hotel — in two hours. Too hot for shopping.*

*Love, Marie*

# Chapter 5

## Auburn, New York
*July 15, 1953*

Dear Carol,

A week from today, I'll be at school again. I'm leaving Auburn on Sunday and hope to stay at the Tatham in New York City, because contrary to my first impression, I'm to receive training in Long Island City rather than Miami. The school there is for those stewardesses who speak Spanish and will fly to South America and the Caribbean area. I don't know which would be worse in July or August — Miami or New York. But I am really excited about everything. I've sent for more radio show tickets, which should solve the evening entertainment problem for a while, but then I may have night homework to do, although I doubt it. School for Pan Am will be like a regular job, I imagine, with regular hours for seven weeks. Training might be hard, lasting 11 hours a day with just one day of rest. I learned that I typically would fly 12-14 days, and once I had logged 65-85 flight hours each month, I would have a break of about 16 days. Our flight schedules could change month to month.

Oh, and I have a month's vacation with pay every year, so that I can take two weeks this January and go either to Miami or the French Riviera, depending on which continent I am on, or I might take the whole vacation and go west as I had wanted to do this summer. It will depend on my work. Right now, I am enjoying a four week's rest at home. I had told you earlier that when I finished school, I was going to become more sociable. So, I've been dating two nice guys, going to the movies, the Lyric Circus, Taughannock Falls, and just plain driving. I had a card from Dot, who's going to – heaven forbid – Borneo now. That's one of the wildest spots on the face of the earth – some parts still unexplored.

Phyllis Storrs dropped a note and explained about her job and the little office all her own, which she is having fixed up. It doesn't look like I'll make it to Keuka with just six days to go and so many things to be done; time is going to whiz by. It won't be any more like it was at school where either Joyce or I could so easily cart things to and fro. I probably won't be home again until my two-weeks remaining vacation next summer.

Write me about your summer and what you are doing. Say hello to everyone.

Love, Marie

# Chapter 6

## Second Week of Training
### July 27, 1953

Dear Carol,

You can't know how I love opening your letters. They're always so newsy and so you. Well, here I am in New York and the second week of school. You'll never guess where I'm staying for the time being — none other than down on 11th Street in Greenwich Village at the old Friendly League, our old stomping grounds. [001]

I thought I had written the Tatham House sufficiently ahead of time for reservations, but the Wednesday before I was to leave, I received a letter from them saying that because of all the conventions, they were filled up for some time to come. In panic, I phoned the Allerton — same story. But good old Mrs. Hall "tucked" me in again, and she was a lifesaver, for I had visions of spending the nights in Grand Central Station. Classes are held at La Guardia Field, though, and commuting is eating up far too much time, so next week I plan to move to an apartment in Forest Hills, right between La Guardia and Idlewild, with three other stewardesses, one of whom is in with me now —

---

001    This is where Dot, Joyce, Marie, and I stayed on a Keuka Field Period assignment while working at the Tuberculosis Association on 34th Street.

Norma Wright from Fort Wayne, Indiana. She is an RN and very nice. They all are.

There are 16 — the biggest class Pan Am's ever had. They're all college graduates who all speak a different foreign language: French, German, Portuguese, or Italian. One girl from Wisconsin was a ballet dancer with the Sadler Wells Ballet until she sustained an injury. Another girl, from Switzerland, was with the Ice Follies until she came to Pan Am.

She went to school with Nicky Hilton of the hotel clan and Liz Taylor's ex. We have others from Columbus, Ohio; Chicago, Illinois; Massachusetts, Connecticut; and Pennsylvania. I'm about the only representative from New York. Some of the unusual names are Artha, Chrystal, and Aija. We don't have a lot in common, but we all share the same excited anticipation of getting our wings, which will be a week from Friday.

We'll begin to fly Rainbows that are regular tourist flights and return in October for training on the double-decker Boeing 377 to learn to fly in the deluxe clipper President and President Special. These are the most luxurious commercial airlines that seat up to 100 passengers with a cruising speed of 300 miles per hour. On these crafts are lounges, a circular staircase connected to the main cabin to a lower-deck lounge where cocktails are served, overhead bins have beds that pull down so passengers can sleep over their seats, bassinets, extended footrests, and a French cuisine meal, and caviar. Orchids and perfume are given to the ladies. A light blue logo is painted on the dinnerware and presidential flight press kits are given to dazzle the passengers.

From then on, we will be flying these exclusively, for new girls keep coming in to take over the Rainbows. Turnover is just under 50% a year, so our seniority should work up fast as for overseas assignments, but we aren't flying there in the immediate future. In a way, I'd like it — you get a living allowance of $270 per month in addition to your regular salary, living expenses are lower, and there is no income tax. On the other hand, you must stick it out for three years with only your 30-day-per-year vacation in the States, or a 45-day vacation in your second or third year for having taken your previous vacation in the country to which you are assigned. It's a bit complicated. I admit that we get 85% discounts on vacation travel when we're here in the States. Isn't that terrific? On some flights, stopovers are short, and you don't get too much of a chance to see the countries you are in, but in some like Johannesburg, you are gone for 23 days with two-day stopovers in each of these ports, among others: Oslo, Stockholm, London, Paris, Beirut, and Johannesburg. This is the most popular run with the girls.

Classes are very well organized and interesting. We have manuals, homework and exams and must practice making announcements in our foreign tongue. Some of the courses are in theory of flight, and we must learn the names of the parts of the plane and the physics involved – passenger psychology, first aid, customs regulations, immigration procedures, health clearance, and how to prepare meals. We have excellent frozen meals, which we eat for lunch. Also, we learn self-defense, how to operate the food cart, how to be first responders and to use the defibrillator, how to handle turbulence, and many other things. We take tours of the different airfields in the New York area.

I forgot to tell you about Fran, a Smith graduate, who made her debut with Pan Am's president's daughter. Just every type of person is in our class. We went to Greenwich Village to see La Boheme last night. No more news from this end. Miss you all.

Love, Marie

# Chapter 7

## Forest Hills, NY
### August 12, 1953

Dear Carol,

Had to send you a short note because there's so much news. First and fore-most, hold on tight. Lili, an international student at Keuka, has decided to marry Russ — and in less than a month, too, on September 6th.

I had a letter from her last week and still can't believe she's really singled one out for keeps. Maybe we can all get together at her wedding —  hope so. I get back from my first real flight, Paris — Rome — Paris — New York, on September 2nd, and so should be able to make it. I'm sure it should be quite a festive occasion, knowing Lili. Yes, my first trip is to Paris, on the 28th of August. We got our wings last Friday, and the company executives who were there at our winging gave us a champagne party after the ceremony. I'm having over a week free before I leave Saturday for London. I suppose I should really call this my first trip, for I'm going along in uniform as an extra crew member and will be working and such, but I "deadbeat" (travel as passenger) back on a deluxe Boeing, and the purpose is chiefly to break us in gradually.

I'll have enough time to do a little shopping and sightseeing in London, too, before I come back. Isn't it all thrilling? I'm being paid a month's salary for just these two flights and a week of vacation from classes. Meanwhile, I've been on the go. To begin with, I was most fortunate in finding what I consider the ideal apartment set-up. Three of the stewardesses are living in a real ritzy section (doorman and all) with Elayne Lassiter. She works as manager of a department store these days from 9 to 9, and with our own conflicting flight schedules, we do a fine job of missing each other. They're all just terrific, too. This way, we have all the advantages of an apartment with none of the disadvantages such as electricity, water, and light bills, laundry, and buying house equipment and supplies. We all have dinner here on Elayne, and all the ex-Pan Am girls who lived here and are married or transferred call this the 6-H Club. What's more, I've been dating none other than Jack Berendes three times in one week. [002]

Also, a doctor, and tonight, I'm having dinner with a Wall Street banker. I can thank the other girls for all these blind dates, and they have even more lined up, so I'm really having a social fling for a while.

Yesterday, four of us went to Jones Beach for the day. One of the girl's fathers was on vacation, so he and her mother went along. Swimming in the ocean is so different from Keuka Lake, and that saltwater lets you burn more easily. I saw my first Great Black-Barked Gull, tell Mr. Guthrie. [003]

What's new up there? Dot's supposed to be in New York now. Said she'd call. Write soon.


Love, Marie

---

002    Jack was Marie's blind date at the Keuka College Junior Prom.
003    Mr. Guthrie was our French professor who liked birding.

# Chapter 8

## London, Paris, Rome
### August 28, 1953

*Dear Carol,*

*My first overseas flight was to Paris, the "City of Lights," and to Rome, the "City of Seven Hills." I wish you had been with me in Paris to sightsee.*

*Today, I saw so many of the places that we studied about and although I ordered poached eggs and was served fried, I have been able to make my French understood. Such fun, and one statue is worth a thousand words. When I was in Rome, I mailed Jenkie[004] a card from the Sistine Chapel because she was interested in Renaissance Art. I also saw the Pantheon and Vatican.*

*Earlier, at a champagne party hosted by the company executives, I received my wings before leaving on Saturday for London as an extra member. I wore my uniform for the first time. In London, I had time to shop and sightsee. Afterwards, I flew back "deadbeat" on a deluxe Boeing to New York, which meant I travelled back as a passenger to the States. I was paid a month's salary for just two flights and a week of classes. I arrived back from this last flight on Thursday.*

---

004    A Keuka housemother

My next flight was scheduled to return to Rome and Paris. I will be gone nearly a week with three days in Paris, then I will have a 16-day rest before flying out again on Halloween, unless I am called out on an unscheduled flight. I'm hoping nothing will interfere because I want to attend Mimi Allen's wedding on October 24, 1953. [005]

On my free time, I'm having quite a social fling. In my last letter, I wrote to you that my housemates are providing me with blind dates. Also, I am getting reacquainted with Jack Berendes. He is a graduate of the United States Merchant Marine Academy at Kings Point. Now, he works as a salesman in New York City. Jack doesn't live far from me, so we are having lots of fun together. We have already dated three times this past week. We saw the movie, From Here to Eternity. Also, I have been meeting lots of his friends from the Merchant Marine Academy. However, he has taken a new job in Philadelphia, so I won't be seeing much more of him. We also visited the old UN building at Lake Success, and Walt Whitman's birthplace. I'm also dating a pilot friend who, currently, is on vacation. We are going to the Gene Autry Rodeo.

What an exciting time I am having when not flying!


Love, Marie

---

005    Mimi Allen was Marie's former roommate for two years.

# Chapter 9

## *Break From Flying*
### *September 6, 1953*

*Dear Carol,*

    *It's my first break from flying. Once I have completed a maximum of 85 flying hours, I am required to take a rest, so I wanted to get a letter off to you. Remember our first day of teaching French at Corning High School in Corning, NY, when we fell asleep at 5 p.m. and didn't wake up until the next morning? We had rented a room from Mrs. Paul, who didn't allow us to keep food in our room, so to save money as college students, we hid our tuna fish, peanut butter, oatmeal cookies, and chocolate cake way back in the bureau drawer. What memories it brings back as I applied for a substitute teaching position to work on my days off!*

    *Since I had some time off now, Phyllis Storrs and I attended Lili Malevich's wedding to Russell Stepanoff. Phyllis and I met at the Port Authority in New York City one morning and took a bus to Passaic, New Jersey, where we had great difficulty locating the church where the wedding was to take place. We were directed to four different addresses all over town, it seemed, before we finally saw about 50 people milling around one of the churches. Lili was late arriving, but when she did arrive, she looked lovely in a little-bit-too-fancy-but-typically-Lili long, white gown.*

She was in her glory because there were photographers telling her to smile and to look this way and that. She loved to have pictures taken. When she spied us, she was so glad to see us. Phyllis and I were glad to be together, as we were the only ones speaking English in the congregation. The wedding lasted about an hour. Her brother, George, who was recently discharged from the service, served as an usher. After the wedding, we formed a reception line. When it came our turn to congratulate Russ, I said, "I didn't know when you brought Lili to Keuka this spring that you were going to marry her." He said, "Neither did I," and Lili laughed. She looked after us personally, as much as she could. She was happy to have us there to represent her college friends.

The reception was a gay affair. About 200 attended the banquet, which was a sumptuous affair; so much food and an orchestra playing polka music. Both of us were asked to dance and it was tiring. When it was time to leave, Lili and Russ gave us a big piece of wedding cake and drove us to the station. They were going to change their clothes, but they still had a night and day of partying before they would leave on their honeymoon to spend two weeks at a lake cabin. Now, they are living with his mother until they can find a place of their own. We made Lili promise to keep us up to date on her activities.

We had a ride back to the city with a friend with whom Phyllis works. Phyllis is going to school part time, likes her job, and is looking for a place to call her own. She wants me to visit her in a few weeks. Her pictures of the wedding will be available soon.

Love, Marie

# Chapter 10

## *Reminiscing*

### October 6, 1953

Dear Carol,

I was just thinking the other day — a perfect prospect for Surprise Holiday — of last year this time, how we were making plans for Field Period and getting excited about going to Corning. Remember, the dean called Surprise Holiday so early we couldn't believe it, even when she'd left the dining room. We didn't even know exactly what we'd do this year. How we inspected our room-to-be at Mrs. Paul's for the first time and went out to dinner with Dot's mother before that hectic ride back to school with Dot at the wheel? Gee, sounds like I'm getting sentimental. Guess it must be the season.

Mother wrote that you and Joyce had been over a few Sundays ago. She felt bad about having to break up just when you got really settled, especially since it was your first time there. But you must tell me yourself how it happened that you were in town — some wedding, I understand, but didn't get the circumstances. Speaking of Dot, how is she? Haven't heard a word from her since graduation except for one measly postcard from Connecticut in which she said she'd be in New York soon and wanted to get in touch. That little monkey, maybe I won't see her for three years, and I sure miss her.

*I hear the dining room at Keuka is complete and that Guthrie's house has been moved. What else is new? I keep watching the Time's weekly magazine section – the new releases column – for our epitaph book.* [006] *Say hello to Mr. Wallis for me when you see him and tell him how excited I am about it – more even than he is, I'll bet. How's the new Frosh class this year? Did Jane Stephens* [007] *come back, and how is Red Jacket* [008] *doing? Don't forget to send me the fall issue, will you? Guess I've asked you enough questions for a while. Now, to bring you up to date on this end of the line: Lili's wedding is first on the list, of course. Well, you can imagine what it was like knowing Lili.* [009] *I sent Jenkie a card from the Sistine Chapel when I was in Rome the first time. She was always so interested, like Mr. Lindy, in Renaissance Art. Wonder how much longer she'll be a housemother at Strong Hall, and is Mr. Guthrie still hunting birds?*

*I got back from my last trip on Thursday, and I go out this Friday to Rome and Paris again. I'll be gone for nearly a week, with three days in Paris this time, then I have a 16-day rest before I go out again on Halloween – unless I'm called out on an unscheduled. That Bermuda trip I made was unscheduled. Hope nothing interferes this time, because as things stand now, I'll be able to attend Mimi's wedding on October 24th. I had a note from her on Saturday, and it's to be a very small affair – no printed invitations even. Jack and I were out by Lynbrook to an engagement party on Sunday and stopped by her house, but Mimi was working the 3 to 11 shift at the hospital. We chatted with her parents and watched a program on TV for a while.*

*Jack has a new job now that takes him to Philadelphia, so I won't be seeing him to speak of after this. I've been seeing lots of his friends from the academy. They're terrific fellows and not at all like the ones who came to Keuka that time. Not that there was anything wrong with them.*

---

006    The book published by our English teacher, Mr. Wallis
007    A prospective student
008    Keuka literary magazine
009    See Chapter 9

*Norma and I went to Radio City a while back, saw Roman Holiday, and had dinner making a real day of it. When are you going to be in this neck of the woods? You have me dying to catch up on all the gossip. Had a note from Barb and a card from Mary from Utah. She went after all. Must write a line to Isy.[010] How has she been? Bet up to her ears in work, the only one of us teaching. Did I take it that you passed your driving test?*

*And, oh yes, what happened to the pictures you took on Class Day? Hope they turned out all right. Would love to see them. Must get supper now.*

*Love, Marie*

---

010     My roommate, Isabel Gamble

# Chapter 11

## *Vacation*
### March 24, 1954

*Dear Carol,*

*I feel just terrible having missed you on Friday. As Elayne must have told you, I was on vacation and spending a few days with some relatives in Haddonfield, NJ. The worst part is that I got back at 2 p.m. that afternoon. You hadn't left an address, but I remembered your saying Keuka kept a room at the Barbizon for Women, where the Keuka staff would stay when they were in town. So, I called them, but you weren't on the register. Then, I remembered you had stayed at the Barbizon Plaza when Isy sailed. Thought you might be there, but no luck again. What was the story? I gather it's spring vacation, and you were lassoing up prospective students — right?*

*I remember exactly a year ago that day I was in New York, too, having my first interview with Pan Am. Did seeing the Big Town again bring back any memories of our Field Period stay that December at the League? I never walk down Broadway, but I smile recalling those nights. Seriously, though, it would have been such fun to meet for dinner and just get caught up. I haven't heard from you since before Christmas — directly, that is. I had a letter from Joyce last week, and she said she didn't know the latest where you were concerned, that she'd read Sue Goodrich had* been appointed to your post but didn't know whether that meant you had made other plans or that the staff in that department was being increased.

So, what goes, hon? Is it to be Florida next year? Joyce also said Mary Smith was supposed to marry in Los Angeles yesterday. Don't know the whole scoop on this. Dottie wrote – finally – while I was away, too. Doesn't sound at all bored, but rather is having a romance in the jungle with some English lumberman. Leave it to Dot! Instead of driving a Cadillac that she drove in the States, she gets around now on a motorbike. I tried to get Lili on the phone as I was passing through Philly last Tuesday, but no answer. She must be working days. Joyce said Rol and she had been down to dinner at Mimi and Bob's, that she brought along a five-inch angel food she'd baked, and that the Ithacans have a new and nicer apartment.

As for me, you've probably heard of all the celebrities I've been having on my flights, so I won't go into that. Oh, yes, I made my first trip to Massachusetts over the weekend. It was quite the spur of the moment, but one of the girls who used to live with me is moving back to Boston. Sunday morning, we had a grand tour of Bean City. We saw the Bunker Hill Monument, Paul Revere's home, the church where he hung the lantern to warn "the British are coming," Beacon Hill, and we went aboard the USA Constitution. Later, we ate a six-course real Italian cannelloni dinner with all the trimmings, and then drove home. Remember the fun we always had on impromptu occasions?

Have you had the time to do much reading lately? I have a book you simply must put on your list, *The High and the Mighty*, which has been on the bestseller list for a long time. It was about a plane trip, the cockpit and cabin reactions – not too technical but so exciting!

My vacation is legally "up," and tomorrow I will be on standby. On Friday, I go out on a 114 – an 8-day flight to Paris and Rome. Just think! I'll make April in Paris! I've been having some wonderful times both here and abroad, too. In the last eight weeks, for instance, I've seen the Jack Kramer Pro Tennis Tour in White Plains and the Barbara Ann Scott Ice Show, but I liked the Follies and Ice Capades better. Then, one night, Jack Berendes took me to see Sabrina Fair on Broadway with Joseph Cotton and Margaret Sullivan, which I loved. Since he was on vacation during February, we caught many of the shows that really speak of the winter months in New York. We also went to the National Cat Show, the Annual Sportsman Show at Madison Square Garden, the International Motor Show, and the Antique Show at Madison Square, too. After that, we ate dinner at Lindy's, no less, and caught the premiere of Liz Taylor's newest movie at Radio City.

In between, there was the International Indoor Amateur Tennis Tourney (as you can see, I'm still a rabid tennis fan), and then I was introduced to the Metropolitan Opera where Robert Merrill and Roberta Peters were starring in The Barber of Seville.

Today, I've been shopping and skating at Rockefeller Center. The temperature was 54 degrees, and the sun was shining, which seemed strange skating under those conditions but nice, with the music and all.

Did I tell you what I plan to do next year when I have a month's vacation? Norma, another stewardess, and I are taking ours together. We want to go to Central and South America — Panama City, Mexico City, Havana, San Juan, Rio de Janeiro, Lima, Caracas, and Columbia being the rough itinerary. Carol, when you get a chance, please send me this year's Red Jacket — just to see how the new editor is performing.

How I have been rattling on! That talk we missed would have been so much more satisfying. What do you hear from Isy? Is she getting married at Easter or waiting until June? Looks as though that much disputed arbitrary list goes like this for the first four: Lili, Mimi, Mary, Isy. Must admit, I was wrong on a few accounts. Let's see, that leaves you, Dottie, Joyce, and me. Let's stick together now! Bye for now, and do write soon.

Love, Marie

# Chapter 12

## London, France, Beirut, Johannesburg
### June 20, 1954

*Dear Carol,*

*It's a lovely Sunday afternoon in Forest Hills. It reminds me of that day like this about a year ago at Keuka. Remember when you and I set out for a leisurely after-church-sunbathing-boating session, drifted somewhat, considerably misjudged our distance and time, and were frantically paddling toward Bluff Point when the dinner bell rang? We were so out of breath, sun-burnt, and in our bathing suits. What fun! Does it seem to you a whole year since graduation? And Carol, do you realize we haven't seen each other in over a year?*

*Joyce wrote to me of your tentative plans for coming to New York, and I'm excited already. Only hope and pray I'll be in from a flight, but I won't know my schedule until July 6th at the latest, even then it's subject to change. Let's hope for the best. Heaven knows we've missed crossing paths too closely in the past. Oh, we'll have such a wonderful three days. I'm thinking of a million things to do, places to go, and sights to see. We'll even outdo that wonderful Field Period.*

*Tell me, how was your trip to Florida? You've got one up on me there, because that's one spot on this earth I have yet to experience visiting. But I've been to Beirut, on one of my recent trips. It's the capital, chief port, and the largest and* oldest city of Lebanon located on the Mediterranean Coast. It is called the "Paris of the East" because of its French influence. It was beautiful and interesting, but I'm glad I'm not based there after all, as conditions aren't good. Over the years, it has had lots of uprisings, and it has a hot and sticky climate. Now, I can add another continent to my list.

I saw Ginger Rogers and her husband at the airport in Paris. She looked quite old and nothing special at all, but then, it was the middle of the night and no one looks their best at that hour. I'm leaving tomorrow on a London-France flight. This will be my first time there since March 1st, a third of a year ago. It seems the seasons just melt into the other. I go out on a trip, and it's winter, and I arrive home and suddenly it's spring. I have an overnight in France this time, so I should have two days for sightseeing and shopping. I've just been on the sundeck at my Forest Hills home. My tan from Johannesburg was beginning to fade, and with dresses showing open arms and backs being in style, I was beginning to look like an albino. I don't know that this beet red is much better but, like the worm, it will turn, I guess.

Remember how dark we were last year at this time, thanks to the sun sessions stolen from chapel exercises? Did I tell you on my ten-day rest, after I flew to Johannesburg, South Africa, "The City of Gold," I took the train to Albany, where my whole family met me? It was Parents Weekend at Rochester Polytechnical Institute where my younger brother, Bob, is a student. We spent the weekend on a jaunt into Vermont and Massachusetts. It was just beautiful, and we had such an enjoyable time with all the family together. We visited Bennington College in Vermont and drove into Williamstown where we saw Williams, a private liberal arts college. On Mother's Day, we drove home, and I had nearly a week there. I entertained the girls from high school days, saw Joyce, and I made the rounds before coming back. It was such a pleasant interlude. How is your brother doing at the University of Florida? Bob made six A's and one B, I hear, so I am quite proud of him.

I went to Brooklyn to see about substitute teaching next year. During our slack season, we have so much time off that there's no reason I shouldn't put it to some constructive and lucrative use. I registered to teach French, English, and grammar school. The next step is to take the respective exams. Everything hinges on whether I'm in town to take the qualifying exams. By the law of averages, I hope to make at least one. I hope I can manage to combine these two professions like other stewardesses do. I must admit that I would like to share my traveling experiences in relation to French and make use of all that preparation, if only I can manage these adolescent New Yorkers. Time will tell. They pay $14 and $15 per day for substitutes; not bad.

Tell me, did you get a chance to read The High and the Mighty? I'm reading The Caine Mutiny now, and that's even better. With all this nice weather here, I won't be hitting the novel much, but while on my Johannesburg trip I read The Fountainhead. I don't mean to sound the easy critic, but this, too, was one of the most enjoyable books I've ever absorbed. About an architect, and on the philosophical side. Think you'd like it — one of those books you remember and want to talk about.

Guess where I was last night? At the stock car races, of all things. Such spills and thrills. Last week, I made it to the harness races at Roosevelt Raceway, and a few days before that, I witnessed my first professional ball game at Yankee Stadium. "Witnessed" was a poor choice of a verb — "sweated through" would have been more appropriate. Such excitement — and the Yankees lost — hurray! I did something, too, that I've been meaning to do for ages, and that is to go through the Lever Brothers Building. We must take it in when you come down — such a monument, and what ideal working conditions and surroundings, nothing but the newest and best efficiency-wise. Well, I'll sign off now.

Love, Marie

# Chapter 13

## News From Forest Hills, NY
### September 11, 1954

*Dear Carol,*

*The day of Hurricane Edna, though all we've seen of it so far is leaden skies and a steady downpour — no winds to speak of yet. Now, they say poor New England will get the full brunt of it again, which doesn't seem quite just, but can you imagine the damage it would cause if it fell on New York City?*

*Well, I suppose you are settling down to another school term. I haven't heard from you since you wrote to wish me birthday congratulations two months ago. Thanks for those and even more so for your long, informative letter and the much-anticipated class day and graduation pictures. Now, it seems to me I've said this before, so maybe I did answer after all. Anyway, it's time we got in touch again. If you only knew how much I long to see you and to spend some time in getting caught up. I came close to it twice recently. Three weeks ago, I was home for a week and attended our high school's fifth class reunion. We had great fun, and for the rest of the week, I was dating more than my whole senior year, I think.*

*Thursday night, my brother and I played tennis until dark, then Joyce came over, and we chatted and watched To Each His Own on TV with Dorothy McQuire, and Carol Joyce is smoking a pipe! Honestly. Rol[011] brought it to her*

---
011    Her boyfriend

*from New York as a joke. Everyone here is switching to them from cigarettes, since that report on the harm of smoking came out. So, the joke's on Rol after all. But really, you must fill one with tobacco mixture and then keep puffing so it doesn't go out.*

*Mother, Dad, and I were planning to drive to Keuka the next day, but Joyce said she thought you would be away that weekend recruiting students. Then, too, I'd have a long talk in French with Mr. Guthrie and see Mr. Wallis and Jenkie, and we wanted to buy some bread at that bakery and to have dinner at the Benham Hotel perhaps. So, I came back to New York in time to go on my next trip to Paris and Rome, from which I returned last Saturday. I had a wonderful time during those six days. I visited Versailles with its Trianons, by Mansard — remember? It is one of the most visited sites in France built by King Louis XIV. Had an audience with Pope Pius XII at his summer residence Castel Gandolfo at the hills outside Rome. Quite an experience! Stopped for the first time on the French Riviera at the airport in Nice, with the Mediterranean lapping the tongue of the runway and had a 20-minute chat with John Steinbeck, though I didn't know who he was at the time; just someone creative and quick on the uptake.*

*Sunday was the semi-finals at the National Tennis Championship being played here at Forest Hills. Jack was coming for me at 12:30 p.m. At 12:15 p.m., Phyllis Storrs*[012] *called. She was in town for a TV show and was calling in connection with an indefinite proposed trip we'd hoped to take to Keuka. Unfortunately, I had to be back Thursday night and, since she didn't want to drive in the Labor Day traffic, that trip was cancelled. She was having her first vacation. Anyway, that night at 8:30 p.m., we just returned from the matches to meet Phyllis and her mother at the door. We had arranged that I would throw a few things in a bag and drive to Willimantic, Conn., with them that night. This we did, and it was such fun. I hadn't seen Phyllis since Lili's wedding, a year exactly from*

012      My college friend

*that day, and her parents since that Class Day when we ate ice cream at their overnight cabin — remember that?*

*Well, Labor Day, I helped them sort and pack some of the eggs from their total of 4,000 chickens. We drove over to her sister's to visit her family; she has three girls now and another on the way. Tuesday noon, we set out for a side trip to the Berkshires. We had Storrs's 1954 Ford, so we had no trouble mechanically, and the radio supplied music when we weren't making our own, singing Keuka songs and such. More fun. We stopped at appealing country gift shops and Stockbridge to see Phyllis's ex-roommate's parents, the Roses. They invited us to stay for dinner at their establishment, which had closed for the summer the day before. That night, we stayed in a motel and had a good night's sleep, though we both brought sleeping bags in hopes that we would be rough-ing it. However, it had rained some and the ground was too damp. We arrived mid-afternoon the next day in Hartford, visited Phyllis's office, and we were invited out to dinner that night at a lovely old place, founded in 1785, that used to be a blacksmith's shop. Meanwhile, we went shopping in H's Fox's.*[013] *After dinner that night, we all went to a summer barn theatre, the Oval Grove, to see a darling musical comedy, Finian's Rainbow. We spent that night at Phyllis's ex-roomie's place in Meriden. Phyllis slept on the couch, and I on the floor in the sleeping bag underlaid with cushions. So, you can see this jaunt cost us next to nothing. Phyl being still a student, and I a struggling working girl, we were both willing to cut corners.*

*I think the territory we covered Thursday en route back to Long Island was some of the most breathtaking yet, especially up around Bethel, Georgetown, and Weston. Some of the homes — pardon me, estates! — reached 6-H*[014] *in time to cook dinner for us. Then, we walked around the neighborhood and the down-street district.*

---

013    A department store that became Filene's
014    My apartment

*Joyce couldn't make it last month. I didn't hear you weren't coming, so I called the hotel where you were planning to stay, but they had no reservation for the two of you. As it was, Phyllis was my first guest. Natalie, my roommate, was out on a trip, so Phyllis slept right here. Next morning, we had a late and leisurely breakfast before she had to leave at noon. I am on reserve standby until tomorrow morning. The weather is so bad; I certainly hope I'm not called out. Did I tell you that I saw The Caine Mutiny Court Martial on Broadway? It was superb, directed by Charles Laughton and starring Lloyd Nolan, Barry Sullivan, and John Hodiak. Guess I could go on and on. When you're down this way again, please call and let me know you're in town. Maybe we'll be synchronized this time. If I'm free for a few days, perhaps I could drive back with you for a short stay. Even so, let me know when you will be at the college during October, so far as you know. Maybe I could get up to Keuka between trips, and we could have another Surprise Holiday. My parents are coming down for a few days in late October or early November. On October 4th and 5th, I expect to take my NYC licensing exams for substitute teaching. I haven't heard anything from them since sending in my application, so hope it was okay.*

*Does Dot have a new address since moving from Sarawak? I had a long letter from Mary Smith, in response to a belated wedding present. She was in Houston and said Barb Tufts[015] was driving down to visit her on her two-weeks' vacation. Also mentioned that she hears regularly from Pat Minor, which was a surprise, and that Pat's father had died this spring. Guess that's all the news.*

*So, your mother has a car! That's fine now that she's located nearer you. Now, I really must go.*

*Love and do write soon, Marie*

---

015      Another Keuka classmate

# Chapter 14

## Christmas 1954

Dear Carol,

Best Wishes for a Happy Holiday Season!

In case I haven't acknowledged those Class Day photos yet, they were so much appreciated. They brought back those last college days so vividly. Not much news. Suppose you heard of my wonderful two-week Scandinavia trip that brought me to Chicago.

Was so surprised about Barb, as I hadn't heard about her tragedy until I called the lab. I visited her in the hospital, and she was in good spirits but hard hit. There had been an explosion in the laboratory where she worked, and she got hurt badly. Her legs were damaged, and she has to wear braces, which she has trouble putting on and off but felt encouraged. It's a long, slow grind. While in the hospital, she had been working five mornings a week at the lab from her wheelchair. After that, I was sent on a temporary three-week relief assignment to Beirut. I took a side trip to Damascus[016] where several stewardesses and I visited a real mosque. Also, we went to a street market and haggled over prices. More fun!

---

016    The capital of Syria in the southwest and a major cultural center of the Arab world, not too far from Jerusalem

*My next trip was to London. FDR Jr. was on board this flight. While there, several stewardesses and I visited the Tower of London and saw two good plays, The Boy Friend and Bell, Book and Candle with Rex Harrison and Lili Palmer. I got back on December 9th, and by then I had accumulated my 950 maximum flight hours for the year. So, I am home in Auburn with the family for the rest of the month. In January, I have my vacation. I plan on spending this month skiing in Austria, so it will be some time before I have another flight. Between times, I've been going through the process of getting licensed to do substitute teaching. After three exams, including an English oral (that was a stickler), I think I am all set now to begin teaching in February, except for a physical. I'm anxious to get started — after all our training and prepa- ration, for the experience and the money, $16 per day, and with the split shifts, I should be through by 1:00 p.m. Then, when I'm in from trips, I've been going to classes a couple of nights a week, just for the fun of it. Guess that about catches me up.*

*How about you? Soon as your new semester's schedule is figured out, let me know it. Sorry we couldn't get together until now, but things just didn't seem to work out. We could have such fun in New York. Let's see, it's been three years since that Field Period, hasn't it? And remember where we were two years ago — eating our peanut butter or tuna fish sandwiches up in that front room of 160 Sly Avenue and hoping Mrs. What's-Her-Name wouldn't smell any peculiar odors, planning those classes until the wee hours? Sure was fun. Remember that silly Christmas play I had to produce? And the faculty dinner we served at, and the Christmas party we went to, and the dinner the Greggs took us to? I'm such a sentimental old gofer once I get started.*

*I just read the latest Alumnae News and was surprised to learn Carmen Egletis is married, and Cyrille is engaged. Ken Pollard, the fellow Beulah Chappell is marrying, was one of my high school classmates. I got Dottie's* birthday card off early. When she finally gets home, we'll have a big reunion. Imagine having your appendix out in Singapore! What do you hear from Isy? Do let me hear from you, say hello to your family, and Merry Christmas!

Love, Marie

# Chapter 15

## January Vacation, Teaching
### February 12, 1955

Dear Carol,

I'm taking a break in the merry-go-round pace, so this is an opportunity to tell you how much I enjoyed our all too short afternoon together during the Christmas holiday. It was so good to catch up on all the Keuka news. It went so fast, and I'm just sorry we didn't have longer, but it was like old times. I only wish we could do it again, soon, and more at our leisure. It was one of the highlights of the Christmas holiday for me.

Betsy Atwater's wedding in Auburn was a lovely affair, and there was a little delegation from her Keuka class. Probably Joyce has told you all about it and Dot's plans for her wedding, too. Or you know more about her wedding-to-be than I, having heard details from her mother yourself. My mother was talking with Mrs. Lawson and passed on word that Brian Casidy[017] would be in the States during April and was planning to stop by the Wingert's in Elmira, and that an August wedding was planned. Does this mean Dot will sever with the missions, and will she be living over there in Borneo indefinitely?

---

017    Dot's fiancé

*I was surprised that Mickey[018] had died. Could you fill me in the details, Miss Kilgallen[019] of Keuka? I had a note from Mr. Wallis the other day thanking me for the Christmas card. Seeing how busy he is, I thought this was extremely sweet, but it seems busy people are the ones who get such things accomplished. Say hello to Mr. Guthrie for me, and was it really Jenkie that we were talking about? What in the world will she ever do? Certainly not just step down and retire, I'm sure of that. Well, after finishing the holidays very pleasantly at home, I embarked on my January vacation. I spent one day in Frankfurt, the main city of Germany, where I visited Goethe's home. Also, I spent four days in Munich, the third largest city in Germany that is also the largest publishing city in Europe that publishes one of the biggest daily newspapers. It also has the largest public broadcasting network. I spent it with a girl I went to school with who is now married to a lieutenant stationed with the Army there.*

*I also stayed 1.5 weeks skiing in the Alpine town of Kitzbuhel, the best ski area in Austria. I also spent four days in the capital city of Vienna, the largest city on the Danube River. It is known as the "City of Music," as Beethoven and Mozart called Vienna home. Sigmund Freud also lived there. Back home, my teaching certificate was awaiting me. I lost no time contacting schools in the vicinity. Right away, the phone started ringing. This is a good substitute time, mid-winter weather, with its colds and flu prevalent.*

*Some mornings, I have had as many as five calls. For substituting, I earn $16 per day, working from 9-12 and 1-3. Not bad, though from the papers, I was prepared for the salary being worst, because I've had the younger grades. So far, I have had no major disciplinary problems. However, the children do leave you slightly hoarse and worn out after a day, with all their squirming. Last week I had the 4th Grade for three days, and I left on Thursday for Paris, but I was back Sunday. Monday and Tuesday, I taught a 2nd grade, and on Wednesday and Thursday, I taught a*

---

018    Keuka's Spanish professor
019    Iconic American journalist, columnist, and media personality

1st grade. The class average is 34, a bit large. Yesterday, I took my purser test. A purser oversees the stewardesses, making sure the passengers are comfortable.

This person writes reports and verifies that the safety procedures are followed. A situation has come up in that they are down to 18 months seniority for this job. It means increased responsibility, headaches, and a larger salary. I mulled over the pros and cons for one week prior to making an application. I took the tour through the UN two weeks ago, which was an hour long and most impressive. A girl I went to high school with is a guide there – her father is a millionaire!

Oh, I did start those oil landscape painting lessons. They last two hours per week every Wednesday night. I'll never be a Picasso, but it's lots of fun. Tell me, now that it's contract time. What did you decide about staying at Keuka? I'll be waiting to hear from you.

Love, Marie

# Chapter 16

## *Update from Forest Hills, NY*
### April 20, 1955

Dear Carol,

   We are having such lovely spring weather, and I can't think of a place I would rather be than at Keuka where spring is something to remember.

   Have you completed your rounds visiting high schools so you can spend time at the college? I guess May Day plans are paramount at this point. I hope the good weather tradition will carry through. I believe the last time we exchanged notes, you were about to sign the contract to renew your stay at Keuka. Don't suppose anything has happened to change your mind. What arrangements have you made about your vacation? Are you going to attend summer school at the University of Florida? Perhaps, if you are coming through New York, and I am in, you could stay with me for a few days. After June 4th, I shall have one room available here, as my roommate Norma is being married that day, and Laurel, another in our number, is leaving in two weeks to be married in California where her home is. Let me know about your schedule, as I plan on getting home a couple of times this summer.

   My brother, Bob, is doing so well at Rochester Polytechnical Institute. He was president of his class this junior year and has been elected president of *his fraternity next year, his last semester. This summer, he will take Army ROTC training in the south, which will be a new experience for him. I am expecting a call any day now from Brian Casidy. Dot said she would have him give me a buzz when he was passing through New York. I am looking forward to meeting him.*

*I was so very disappointed that our little reunion didn't work out in Hartford. I got in from a trip that Friday morning all excited about the idea, even had a ride, roundtrip, held up for Friday night and Sunday afternoon that we could drive over to visit Mimi Mitchell in Amherst, Massachusetts. Then, Phyl's letter arrived that your plans had been changed. So, I hopped a train to Trenton, NJ, and visited an old grammar school through high school days friend of mine, who is married now and living in Levittown, PA. We had a nice time chatting. She has a boy, 2, and a girl, 7 weeks old. I got the cook's tour of that historic region.*

*Thanks so much for the Red Jacket, Carol, but whatever have they done to our little magazine? Probably the poor kids had their appropriation cut again — but only one issue a year now. And the material didn't seem up to standard to me, but then maybe we're prejudiced, huh? Right now, I am looking forward to the next Alumnae News, as I understand it features our class, and we'll be brought up to date on everyone.*

*I mentioned the wedding I'm to be a bridesmaid in, which I am making my own gown for. First time I've fooled around with sewing in some time, but everything's going fine so far. Do you remember the other girl I was in a wedding for our sophomore year? Well, Jo just had her third child the day after St. Patrick's Day, so she is calling her Patricia; isn't that cute? I've been put on our President's special flights, which leave New York once a week, one to Paris, one to London. This is our most deluxe flight, service course by course on Rosenthal China, entrée choices to include lobster, filet mignon, and roast partridge "from the mountains of Tibet," etc., but what intrigues me most is the tray cart of cherries we roll down the aisle between dessert time and cordial* service. There are five of us aboard to serve a maximum of 40 passengers, so the only undesirable part of the whole setup is the quick turnaround back to the States.

I miss not spending more time overseas. Supposedly, this arrangement is for April only, but at least I've been getting to London. Saturday and Sunday was gorgeous. All the hit New York plays are running over there. They are much cheaper and easier to get into. I saw Cinerama Saturday night there, and I hope to see Kismet on my next trip. On Sunday, several of us went to St. Paul's,[020] and we went sightseeing in the afternoon. I still have so much to see over there.

Until now, I have been regularly teaching, but with the weather so nice, the teachers' attendance is stable, too, so from now until June, I don't expect many calls. During January, February, March, and early April, I was constantly being called — three, four, even five times a day sometimes — and subbed for everything from kindergarten through 8th grade. I heard from mother that Joyce now has the family car as her own. That must be a wonderful convenience. I've been thinking of investing myself before the summer is over. Joyce and Rol flew down to New York for the Easter Parade. Norma, my housemate, wanted to go, this being her last year in NY.

Wouldn't it have been a scream if we'd met on the avenue? As it was, our paths didn't cross. Did I tell you of the old landscape painting hobby classes, in which I'm enrolled? However, classes have ended for the winter term, and I'm not re-enrolling for the spring term as there is too much going on.

I have a bad case of writer's cramps at this point, so will sign off. Hope to hear from you soon. Give my regards to everyone at Keuka.

Love, Marie

---

020    A famous church constructed by the Jesuit architects' Baroque style in the 1600s

# Chapter 17

## Beirut, The Hilton Charter, Atlantic City
### June 27, 1955

Dear Carol,

I'm just back from my latest trip to Beirut and found your card here this morning. I was sort of standing by a week ago, Saturday, for a call from you, in case you were passing through. Believe this was the date you mentioned when we were at Keuka, and I was home. Gee, I wish we could have some time together again somewhere!

Since seeing you recently, Carol, so much has happened. First, my roommate, Norma, was married June 4th, and I was a bridesmaid. She was at Annapolis during June Week until the night before the wedding, and I was left with all the details — calling to check on caterer, cake woman, photographer, church arrangements, hotel reservations, guest arrivals, rehearsal time, and a few other things. What happens but I get a call to fly on a trip with only five hours' notice on Tuesday morning, and I am not back until Friday morning. Fortunately, I had my gown all done but for a yard of hem and the pressing. I didn't get much rest, with Norma up bright and early on zero day and presents arriving every few minutes. But we had a good day, and the wedding went off well. We had a small reception at 6-H following the ceremony, and

I met a fellow graduate of Harold's, the groom, whom I've dated a few times since.

My next big event was flying on that Hilton Charter flight you no doubt read about. Conrad Hilton was opening a new hotel in Istanbul, the largest city in Turkey. He leased two of our ships to transport a slew of celebrities over there. We worked hard and they drank a lot, but I haven't been so excited in ages due to all the publicity and thrills. Everything was super deluxe – the food, gifts, and service. Here are some of the Hollywood celebrities we had on board: Irene Dunne, Merle Oberon, Sonja Henie, Ann Miller, Mona Freeman, Diana Lynn, Tex and Jinx, Hedda Hopper, Louella Parsons, Keefe Brasselle, Nicky (Liz Taylor's ex), Conrad, John Cameron Swayze, John Considine, and the Warren girls, plus newsmen galore. It was quite a shindig.

When I arrived back from that trip, I was given a publicity assignment to represent the company at a convention in Atlantic City, all expenses paid, of course, so nothing was too good. This was quite an experience, as I had never been here before, and I had a grand time with all that ocean, sunshine, seafood, and men. There were girls there from all the major airlines and it was fun meeting them and comparing notes. I was there only two full days, and I flew home via Eastern Airlines. Yes, I was so delighted to be in when Brian Casidy called. You know, it was strange – only 10 minutes before the phone rang, I opened my desk drawer and noticed Dottie's letter. I must have missed Brian, I thought, because I had been gadding about so.

At first, I didn't realize who that "veddy" British accent could be. I quickly cancelled a dinner date for that evening, and he came out to Forest Hills. He's younger than I thought, but so easy-going; I can see how he and our gal hit it off. You know how set Dot is in what she wants. Did he tell you how they met? It was a hot day, and I supplied him with a beer and, as you must have, plied him with questions, too. We walked around and saw some of the nice homes here, then we went into town to dinner and a show. Brian said he wanted to store up on culture and civilization for the next three years in the jungle. We ate at a place that specializes in Armenian food. We had the most divine shish kebob, and I recognized two celebrities there – Johnnie Ray and Don Budge, a tennis great. Following this, we saw the new musical about the Amish, Plain and Fancy. I remembered that Dot's grandfather was from this locale and that she had done her freshman commentary on it, so Brian was made to take back to Borneo the program with what started out to be a note and ended up a short letter inscribed thereon, all the while protesting about overweight baggage, as it was.

My brother was in town the day I got in from my last trip. He was between finals and ROTC training in North Carolina, so we had one evening together. He came out to Forest Hills and saw where I lived. Then, we stopped in a little Italian place for pizza and finally, we had dessert at Jahn's that has been written up in many magazines, so perhaps you already know about it.[021] When you walk in, you think you have been transported back a century; it's like that, with Victorian décor of hanging lamps of colored glass and beaded strings. The Kitchen Sink Sundae comes in a container that I can only compare to the Davis Cup. It costs about $6 and contains about a gallon and a half of ice cream, not to mention all the trimmings. It serves four people. Bob ordered one of their super sodas, which came in a vase that must have held two quarts of ice cream and real strawberries, too. It did my heart good to see him eat it up.

Please write me soon and let me know about your University of Florida classes and your social life. I'm so very glad you're there after all. And just think – working on your Masters! It sounds so impressive! I have been reading more of Scott Fitzgerald, my old friend. Sorry, but I don't even have my schedule for July yet. I will have to let you know later if I can come to Gainesville for a visit. Mother and Dad are celebrating their 25th anniversary on August 19th, though, and I'm going to try hard to be home for that.

---

021     Jahn's was an old-fashioned ice cream parlor and family restaurant and was famous for its huge Kitchen Sink Sundae.

I visited Joyce's relatives on a recent visit to London. "Who is this rich old man from the Locomotive she's dating?" Brian just let this fall in the conversation. I said, "Rol?" and he said, "No, not Rol." I'm so glad it's the good old summertime again. Thanks for giving Brian such explicit instructions on my behalf. Have fun down there, and I'll be in touch with you again soon.

Love, Marie

# Chapter 18

## Lisbon, London, Germany
### July 27, 1955

Dear Carol,

I'm going to start this letter to you now, though probably I won't be able to finish it in one sitting. Since last writing you, I did manage to get home from a wonderful Lisbon trip, the capital of Portugal, where I spent three full days and two nights. I visited an old castle and palace at Sintra, which is a major tourist destination famed for its picturesqueness, and I spent one day at the famous resort Estoril, which is on the ocean, 36 minutes from Lisbon. It's quite a tourist spot with luxury hotels, beaches, and a casino. I got a nice tan. There was a fair going on and someone was nice enough to drive me to Montserrat, a pretty drive from Lisbon through the countryside, where we got lost in the botanical gardens. It is called "The Emerald Isle of the Caribbean" because of its resemblance to coastal Ireland. Many of its residents are of Irish descent.

I landed in New York at 4:30 on a Friday morning, and since I had a week until my next trip, I called Pan Am to see if I could go home. They are busy, and like us nearby, but they said yes, I could go. I didn't know if things might open in August, and because it was my birthday and so hot here, I left by plane that afternoon. I had a great time every minute at home. I went swimming on a double date, played golf for the first time, and entertained at a roast. Then, Monday noon, at lunch, Pan Am called and said to get right back to New York to take a trip to fly out the next day. I had a 50% discount ticket on American Airlines, and because one passenger too many showed up, I was off-loaded on the flight out of Syracuse, with the result that I didn't get off until three hours later, and I had to go to Newark instead of LaGuardia, just a stone's throw from Forest Hills. Things were hectic, but I made it back to the airport with a hair's margin. However, it was too close for comfort.

Fortunately, we had an exceptionally fine crew that trip. I spent one afternoon and evening in Heidelberg, Germany, which has the oldest and most famous university town, founded in 1386. I visited the castle there and had dinner at the home of "The Student Prince." Karl Franz was the Prince sent to the University of Heidelberg to improve his social skills. Also, there was an operetta set there. Then, in London, the steward and I took a 2½ hour excursion boat trip up the Thames River past Kew Gardens to Richmond, a quaint and picturesque typical English town. In a musty, colorful little book shop there, I found an old book I've been looking for over a year now. I had Earl Wilson, the columnist, aboard my flight coming back, and yesterday I read in his write-up for that night a reference to his Pan Am trip where he mentioned the stewardess. Actor Diana Lynn was with us coming back Monday. She's not very striking.

When do you finish at the University of Florida, Carol? Has it been very hot down South? I think the weather must be breaking all records in New York. I've been trying to keep cool by doing such things as packing a picnic lunch and taking off for the whole day to Candlewood Lake near Danbury, Connecticut. It's beautiful up there, and five of us just swam and basked in the sun. They have a tower diving board, and the water's so clear and clean. The beaches around here are dirty and crowded. One night, three of us went *into Central Park to hear the outdoor Guggenheim Concert at the Mall. It was cool enough for a sweater, and just so enjoyable that we want to do it again soon. Radio City Music Hall has a terrific program on now. Mr. Roberts is the movie, which is excellent, and this new Jack Lemmon really stole the show — and those Rockettes. If there were only reincarnation, I'd love to have been a Rockette for a while, too.*

*Yesterday an engineer I know and I left early in the morning and drove into Pennsylvania. We stopped off mid-afternoon at the farm of some people from Auburn that I hadn't seen in 16 years. They have bought a Pennsylvania Dutch farm, all stone, that is over 200 years old. It has all sorts of lovely trees and different birds around, a barbecue pit, barn, springhouse, and, best of all, a newly completed, spring-fed $8,000 pool that is so big they have a boat to get around in it. They invited us to dinner (homegrown plump chicken) and to stay overnight, but we had to leave to get back to New York by midnight.*

*Today is overcast and soon as I sign off, I am leaving to play tennis with that Jack. He's very good and in a tournament at Beth Page. He won his first round the other day, and we met so many nice people. I get a workout, too, before, after, and in-between. But enough of my activities. I called Joyce when I got home, but she was just leaving for Chicago to visit Barbara Tufts on her vacation. Since then, I've had a letter from her with an account of her time there and the big news, which you no doubt have heard by now, that Mary Kim[022] is expecting about Thanksgiving time. And she always said she never wanted any children. But then, she did say she'd name a girl Stephanie and a boy Steven, didn't she? Bet she'll be a wonderful mother, crocheting, knitting, and cooking for her little "bambino." Wonder which of us — you, Joyce, or I — will throw a bombshell in the way of some announcement?*

*By the way, I have my transfer to California to be officially effective September 1st, so any time after that I could be moving. Thanks so much for*

022    A Keuka colleague

the birthday card. It was so good hearing from Mimi and all the kids, though I was surprised not to hear from Phyllis. She owes me at least one letter and is usually so good about remembering anniversaries and, though busy, ordinarily manages to get a letter off occasionally, but I haven't heard from her since February.

About August, Carol, you know how I'd love to make a visit with you, but with things the way they are, you'd better go ahead and make your own date and plans. Then let me know what's what, and I'll see if I can do it, but I am not very hopeful. I must write Isy one of these days, and I will send a present anyway up to the college, so let me know what type of shower it will be. You know, we never really appreciated those casual "coffee breaks" when we were all together those years, did we? Have you thought what you'll send Dot for her wedding? I want to get my gift off within the next few days. What is the exact date again, do you remember when in September? Was it the 25th?

I must run now. Will you be in New York coming home from Florida? I am scheduled to fly out on August 5th and be back the 8th, so let's try once more to get together. My number is 803-3927, and I'd so love to meet you for a bang-up luncheon and afternoon. I have just loads of ideas of things we could do, but probably it would be best to just talk, and that is usually what we do when we're together. I want to hear all about this summer and Florida.

Love, Marie

# Chapter 19

## *Carol's Secret*
### *August 5, 1955*

*Dear Carol,*

*I am going on a trip in a few hours, but I have a ride to the airport, so I want to answer your most welcomed letter which just arrived an hour or so ago. Thank heavens you told me the big secret, and I'm so honored you told me first. You really threw a bombshell, and I'm glad, so very happy about it all and hope everything turns out all right. You must be certain that he is the one, or you never would have put your tentative plans down on paper, but just as soon as everything is definite, be sure to let me know right away, and I'll see what I can do about getting my vacation, so as to be at your wedding. You know I wouldn't miss it for the world. Do you think it will be in June? Gee, I wish I'd hurry up and find someone, too. I'm afraid I'm too hard to please — I will probably end up being "Aunt Marie." Heaven forbid.*

*Here we are at 24 — or I am, at least, and would like to start to work on those "dream children" — me and Charles Lamb! But it's you we'll be talking about. Be sure to bring along a picture of Hubert. I'm dying to see him. That will certainly help your French. And going there next summer! Do you think you'll fly, or go by boat? After that French Civilization course, you'll feel as* much at home in Paris as Penn Yan. And wait until Mr. Guthrie hears! Oh, Carol, I'm so excited! And it really looks good for our getting together this time. If you leave Florida on the 11th, does that mean you'll be here on the 12th? If you could just drop me a card, I'll stick around the phone about that time. I wouldn't want to miss you by going to the A & P! Do you think you could stay over a day or two?

I must run soon. I heard from Mimi Mitchell the other day that her father died last week. It was quite a shock, as that sort of thing always is, but Mimi says they wouldn't want him back to have him so uncomfortable as he was the past few years. Her mother must feel lonely nights, so I'm going to try to get out to Long Island. Maybe the two of us could go when you're here, provided we have more than one day. Keep your fingers crossed. I hope they don't throw a Bermuda at me. I'm on standby Saturday from 4 p.m. on, but that's all right. This secret is going to be hard to keep, but I'll do it. I can't wait until next week. All for now.

Love, Marie

# Chapter 20

## Transfer To California
### August 13, 1955

Dear Carol,

I stayed by the phone all day yesterday hoping you'd call and could stay over for a few days. What happened? Did you go right through? I sent you this letter over a week ago from the airport. Didn't have your letter there and guess I gave the wrong box number, as it came back on Wednesday. I'm leaving Tuesday for the coast. My transfer came through earlier than expected. I have from the 30th to get there by the 12th for classes in San Francisco. It looks as though I'll be leaving New York about September 1st. I'm flying to California, as it will only cost me $50 half price, TWA, stopping a few days each at Dayton, Ft. Wayne, and Detroit to visit friends. I'm quite excited. These are such busy, full days! So, it will be "back to school" in September again.

I had fun browsing through the August *Mademoiselle* college issue to see all the college fashions. I had a letter from Dot earlier in the week, full of her plans. She hopes we can get together when I'm on the coast, in Manila or some place. I don't know, but it's a nice thought. Do keep me posted, Carol.

I'll write you my address as soon as I have one. Meantime, write me here in New York and the mail will be forwarded. Sorry we flubbed this last chance for a get-together in New York City. Be good now.

Love, Marie

# Chapter 21

## San Mateo, California
### October 24, 1955

Dear Carol,

    At long last, an evening free to have a chat with you. It's been such an eventful and adventurous two months since leaving New York. I will do my best to brief you on them later, but first, your last letter, which I received just before leaving. It was such a nice send-off. How are things on campus this year? Were you able to make it home for your birthday after all? Did my card reach you on time? Things were so hectic about then, moving and all. Do tell me how you spent it and all the latest concerning you and Hu. I'm dying to know what's happening in the romance department. Joyce wrote that you two had spent a weekend together and says you are as much up in the clouds as Isy was our senior year. And how are Isy's plans progressing? The wedding is so close now with December just a month away. Have they set a definite date yet, and what are your gowns like? You could write a full letter just on that.

    Coming out to the coast, I had two weeks in which to visit friends in the Midwest. I stopped off in Dayton, Ft. Wayne, and Detroit and had a grand time. I told Dot of how we ran across the grave of Johnny Appleseed in Ft. Wayne, as Dot had written her freshman commentary on him. He was a very religious person, so I could see, as a Christian education major, why she wrote about him. I have a colored slide of it which came out beautifully. I hope someday to be able to show you some of my slides — not that I have so many or that they're very expert, but at any rate they represent a spotty chronicle of my travels. Then, in Chicago, during a two-hour transit, I talked with Barbara Tufts at work, so she is back on her job full time now, but with the Lodges who got her the job leaving, I can't understand why she stays.

Since then, I've had a note from Mary Kim. I would have visited her, too, except TWA doesn't land anywhere near her. Upon arriving in San Francisco, with its Chinatown, cable cars, Nob Hill, Golden Gate Bridge, and Top of the Mark — such a colorful, lively, and cultured town — I had a few days to orient myself before classes began. They lasted for two weeks, then I had a week off before my first trip, a 15-day flight to Singapore, with layovers in Honolulu, Wake, and Manila as well. Had a ball along the line. Singapore is a shopper's paradise! Wish I could completely surprise you now with the news of my rendezvous with Dot in Manila, but no doubt you've heard all about it from Joyce or Mrs. Wingert, or Dot herself by now, as it happened the 5th of October, almost three weeks ago. Carol, it was more than a coincidental 5,000 to 1 shot. When I think of all the variables, of how Dot and Brian were only in Manila overnight and that I was there, too, at the same hotel, for the very first time. I was nearly diverted to Tokyo, and our planes were five hours late. (If they had been two hours later, I would have missed them completely.) When I think of all these obstacles, I am convinced Providence was smiling upon us in that remote and exotic part of the world. You can just imagine what a reunion we had, not having seen each other since gradua-tion. Knowing Brian already, I didn't feel like such an intruder waking them up at 5:30 a.m. on their honeymoon. He was certainly a peach to put up with all that women talk. I wonder if we can all get together in 1957, or whenever they get back — sure hope so.

As for living in California, it's all they make it out to be. I'm living with three other girls in a home of our own in a lovely residential suburb about 10 miles from San Francisco called San Mateo. We visited the campus of Stanford and the famous chapel with the lovely mosaic art. Going through Atherton on the way down, we looked up Shirley Temple's home. It's not nearly so impressive as I'd thought it would be. She only lives about 12 miles from here. We're on the verge of a strike, as perhaps, you've read. At our union meeting last week, we voted for it, and so I had to support the decision by walking in the demonstration line, with signs carried and all. The mechanics, ground service, commissary, and flight service are all in it together, so we had a showing of well over a thousand at the airport that day. I'd as soon have walked down the street naked, but what can you do?

That night, there was a picture (I was right behind them) of two of my ex-roommates from New York in the picture. Just another of my weird experiences — more fun! Wednesday midnight is the deadline, so what will come of it all, I don't know. I have applied for my teaching license, but evaluations take so long. I have had 10 days off so far, and I am not scheduled for another flight this month, though I am on standby a couple times this week. After my next trip, I am going down to San Fernando to visit my aunt and uncle. I am going to stay a week or so, and perhaps I will be there for Thanksgiving. When I wrote Mrs. Wingert about Dot's plans, she mentioned your being there that day of the wedding and how she hated to see you leave. Did you get to see Phyllis Storrs when you were there?

Hope to hear from you soon.


Love, Marie

# Chapter 22

## Teaching, Japan, Hong Kong
### April 27, 1956

Dear Carol,

Gee, it's been a long time since we chatted, hasn't it? But I received your thoughtful St. Patrick's Day card and note with so much pleasure, and here I am throwing the ball back to you. I am teaching 7th grade at my favorite school again today. It is 8th period, homeroom time, and the students are all busy trying to finish up homework before going home. I've been home almost two weeks, since my last trip to the Orient. I learned to water ski at Wake Island, a great sport, and I was in Japan during Cherry Blossom Time. I had a suit made of raw silk. Imagine this at less than 350 yen, and $1 per yard! I cut out a photograph from Vogue, which the dressmaker duplicated to perfection, corroborating that old Japanese attribute of "adopt, adapt, adept." I met actor Louis Calhern and Marlon Brando's secretary. (They were in the lobby, as they and Marlon Brando were staying in the same wing of the Imperial Hotel as we.) He was in Japan along with Calhern and Glenn Ford for the filming of Teahouse. Mr. Mayer and Mrs. Samuel Goldwyn were passengers to Hong Kong in connection with the Guys and Dolls premiere.

In Hong Kong, I had my first ride in a rickshaw, and I ate dinner in true oriental fashion a la chopsticks. There was much sightseeing, as you can imagine, and shopping for the bargains are many and great. Also, I read 2½ books that trip. The other day, I read *Bonjour Tristesse* by that (at the time it was written) 18-year-old French girl. Didn't think too much of it.

I enjoyed your account of Keuka these days. Three whole years since we were wrapped up in all those graduation activities! And a good year since I've seen you. Well, I'll be home for the greater part of the month of June. I'm stopping off in New York for some plays and shopping and to see my NY friends there on route to upstate. Then, the 8th, Bob graduates from RPI on a Friday and our family, perhaps together for the last time in some while, plans to take part of the next week for a vacation drive through New England to Maine. It sounds like a great month lined up, and one of the big red-letter days will be when we get together for a good old chit-chat. I want to hear the latest of your plans with Hubert – and to tell you of his (I think) counterpart in my own life! I'm not too sure about all this – it's an entirely new sensation, or should I say "state," to me – and it seemed to have happened so fast. Well, we'll see.

The other night, I saw *Man in the Gray Flannel Suit* – excellent cast and timely theme; sort of a later-day *Best Years of Our Lives*. Not too long ago, I finally caught up with Disney's *2000 Leagues Under the Sea*. Since I translated the book for one of our French classes, I was interested to see how they handled it. Then, there is *Picnic*. Have you seen it? It really captures the small-town atmosphere. Very good. There have certainly been some good movies made this past year. I picked all the major winners at the Academy Awards last year. It's sad that I'm not a betting woman. This James Dean was certainly a sad loss, wasn't he? Boy, what a talent! I am anxious now to see him, Liz, and Rock Hudson in *Giant*. What a combination!

It's now Saturday morning, and last night I had a date to see Silk Stocking in San Francisco with Don Ameche and the original New York cast. It was fair. Tonight, I have a dinner date with the same fellow, and this afternoon one with a bachelor teacher for tennis, but it's not like being with your best date. I'm finding out everything seems rather hollow when you're just filling in. I've had my car over two months now and do so enjoy the convenience of it.

When do you make the break with Keuka, and what are your plans for the summer? I understand Isy will be home for a while in June. Bob, my brother, has accepted a job with Alcoa at $430 a month, which is darn good starting pay and with a company that has a great future, it would appear. This flying around for interviews at company expenses during spring vacation reminded me of that phase in our own careers. Well, Carol, I will sign off for now. I leave here on Memorial Day and would love to hear just a line from you about that possible June reunion. So long for now.

Love, Marie

# Chapter 23

## Southern California, Singapore
### August 21, 1956

Dear Carol,

This is a quick note to seal in with your birthday greeting. Hope you get it all right at this address. Send me your new box number when you're all settled. I'll be interested in knowing how you're getting along. I know you must be very busy but in a wonderful way. You'll never guess where I first heard about your graduate assistantship at the University of Florida coming through – in Singapore! Yes, after returning from Dot's and Brian Casidy's reunion. Did you get copies of those pictures? I treasure them. I flew back TWA on the day of their collision with Quantis Airlines in the Grand Canyon, over which scene of the crash we must have unbeknownst flown just a few hours later. Then, first chance I had, I requested a Singapore trip and left the 5th of this month.

Dot and I had just about a full day together, and we made the most of it, as you can imagine. She looks just great – thinner than I've ever seen her – and at this stage of her pregnancy, she is full of the old bounce. She and Brian met me at the airport on the evening our flight got in, and I stayed at the house they are leasing, servants and all. It's a lovely, spacious place on the outskirts of town and because help is so cheap, Dot is truly a lady of leisure. She and Brian are so cute together — just like newlyweds, after almost a year together — good to see. They are still up in the air as to what the future holds for them.

Well, I'm back from that trip now and with two weeks off, so before school begins, I am finally taking that tour of Southern California. The town I'm stopping over in tonight is the quaintest, most picturesque Danish community (70%) I just happened to stumble on. They wear native garb, speak with the tongue of the mother country, and sell their own craft, etc. They, also, serve Danish food, and I had "fukadiller" (Danish meat balls) for dinner. Within the last two years, it's been discovered, I understand, and now caters to the tourist trade. Also, it's a very wealthy community — gateway to the Santa Ivey Valley, near Santa Barbara. There are 21 millionaires living in the environs, I was told. Tomorrow, I hope to take in Disneyland — great fun, just me and my VW, but after being so closely associated with passengers and "people" for over two weeks solid, I relish the solitude and change.

Carol, thanks so much for your remembrance of my birthday. I enjoyed your letter as always, and the card was just darling. I've been so busy since coming back — keep thinking of things to tell you. I had the actor Gene Tussey on my flight coming into San Francisco for the convention the other day. He was with his family, who were all very nice. Before that, I had Rex Hartwig, a big name in the Australian tennis world, and I'd seen him play many times and Harry Owens, an orchestra leader and TV personality in the West. I manage to read about an average of one book a trip.

How was the Keuka reunion with Bobbie Lewis, and all? Bet you had a ball. It's been four years since we were leaving for our senior year. Trite but true — it doesn't seem possible. Sure enjoyed the Alumnae News the other night. I sent it on to Dot, as she mentioned not receiving it. Really must send in a contribution soon to that Alumnae Fund. Just the news alone is worth it. I love to keep up with everyone. And speaking of "keeping up," now that Dot's been away for three years, she really couldn't get over the disposable diapers I brought along for the baby-to-be. They are busy trying to choose a suitable one-syllable name for it, but we weren't able to hit on one when I was there, even with all my suggestions. Also brought Dot some of those button earrings with the change-it-to-match-your-outfit Snap-On caps — have you seen them yet? Sure are novel, and she got a big kick out of them.

Dot, incidentally, has turned quite domestic, having made her own maternity smock — very smart, striped affair. She never got around to seeing a doctor until a few weeks ago in her sixth month. Her mother really chewed her out about it, but Dot says the doctor says she's in great shape. Her mother's letter arrived while I was there, telling of your news — your graduate assistantship at the University of Florida — and once again let me say how happy I am everything worked out so well for you to this point. Keuka will have been good experience to have under your belt, don't you think? Do keep me posted as to your love life if you'll excuse that term. I'll do the same if anything should develop here of note. Must run now.


Love, Marie

# Chapter 24

## *Waikiki Biltmore, Honolulu*
### *November 11, 1956*

*Dear Carol,*

*I've been carrying your last letter around for the last few trips, but I simply am not the correspondent I used to be. Anyway, especially here with the balmy breezes and sunny skies, it's hard to realize that Thanksgiving is less than two weeks away and Christmas is just around the corner from there. That will be the time for hearing from everyone, I suppose, for busy and scattered as we all are, that's one sin we'll never be guilty of, let's hope. Not keeping in touch, at least, that one time of the year! Well, if I had been a prompter writer, I could have caused this letter to positively sparkle, what with the news of Mimi's expecting and my two visits with Dottie, but suppose by now that news has seeped through the grapevine.*

*After vacation and learning of the Casidy's temporary stay in Singapore, I requested and received a trip there. I believe I wrote you of that on that birthday card of late August. Then, last month, another trip came along, and we had another reunion! It was Brian's birthday the next morning, so we went shopping for the celebration, and Dot had just been to the doctor that a.m. She weighed less than before conceiving, and as everyone knows, ordinarily* there is a weight gain during pregnancy of 20-some-odd pounds! The doctor told her the baby might be expected the next week! Nevertheless, when the double-dating foursome of us went swimming that evening, guess who was the first in and last out of the water? What a gal! After much discussion, she and Brian had settled on prospective names for their offspring – Mark (my suggestion for a boy), and Anne Elizabeth for a girl. By now, the baby is no doubt a reality, and I'm so anxious to hear all their plans for the future. The day after I left, they were expecting word concerning that Vancouver job, and were that to come through, they would no doubt leave for London in December, and from there to the United States. Can you imagine what it will be like for Dot after more than three years away? So many gradual changes we ourselves are unaware of in food, clothes, cars, building, etc.

I believe I mailed your card somewhere along the way of my southern California tour. I've been promising myself that little jaunt all year and then, with school in the offing, it seemed the perfect opportunity. I drove my VW and just took off alone, since everyone else was tied up, it seemed. I hit Santa Barbara, an enchanting Danish settlement called Solvang that took me right back to Scandinavia, La Jolla, Laguna Beach, Disneyland, San Juan, Capistrano, Knott's Berry Farm and Ghost Town, Palomar, and San Diego. I saw a good deal of California, and it is a grand state. Do hope you'll be able to visit me out here one day soon. I so enjoyed your letter with news of your schedule, classes, living conditions, etc. Have you decided yet on the thesis? I don't quite understand just where a choice is involved. Isn't one mandatory for a master's degree?

As to you and Hubert, I can understand better than you think. You no doubt remember my alluding to a similar relationship, or at least as close to one as I have yet approached to that sort of thing. I was, and am, very fond of John, and I've no question as to his loving me, but when he began talking marriage, we had to take stock of the situation, and there just weren't enough pluses.

Lately, our schedules haven't been coinciding at all, so we don't see too much of each other, and I've never stopped dating other fellows. He has decided to transfer because of all this to Seattle, and though I'll miss him, I do think it's not a bad decision.

What did you think of the elections? That more than once, the night of the returns, of the '52 campaign and the big stir at Keuka, with the torchlight parade and all, remember? If you weren't one of the staunchest Stevenson supporters, there's no one could say you weren't one of the most vociferous, if you'll excuse that 25-cent word. Those were fun times, all right, but so are these. Nevertheless, what with all the wedding presents and baby gifts I've been issuing of late, I can't help but think it's time to settle down, the fling over any day now, with my share of the yoke of responsibility. But somehow you don't much consider that state without someone specific in mind, hmm?

Do you see much of Kim? Having him so near and with your dad, too, must make it cozy when you all get together. How is your mother taking it, and how is your grandmother getting along? My brother, Bob, left his job on October 20, to spend about 10 days at home vacationing, then he went back to RPI for an alumni weekend before driving on to Washington. He was there for a few days being shown the town of his roommate, and they both crossed the Virginia border to Ft. Belfour and a two-year hitch with Uncle Sam. Hard to imagine him a Lieutenant! On January 25th, the lease on our house expires and under the circumstances, we are splitting up. My roommates and I, of the original three, two are married and expecting, and their replacements are so unsure of their plans, we don't want to saddle ourselves with another lease, so it looks like I'm in for a change of address again. Such a nomad life, but change is growth, I philosophize. I am about to bid for my 1957 vacation for July as my first choice. This time, I am considering going home Pan Am via Los Angeles, Guatemala City, for a couple of days there and Panama for three days or so, then to Miami, where I have a friend, for a couple of days.

Will you be in Florida in July or August, or what are your plans? I guess Gainesville is some distance from Miami, isn't it? But if you will be there, I'd love to see you, and I could maybe arrange a side trip there. Then on to Washington for a couple of days via National Airlines to visit friends. I will fly National Airlines to NY and spend a day or two with the old gang there. Then, on home for a good two weeks before going cross-country via TWA or United. We get 50% discount with them and 90% on Pan Am and National, so the long way around won't cost anymore, and it would be different and a good chance to see some of Latin America. There is so much that I would like to do and see, it's hard to choose. Let me know if you'll be in the south this summer.

What do you hear from Isy? She becomes a mother this month, if I remember correctly. Aren't she and Ron somewhere near Illinois now? Let's see now what there is to tell you of my trips of late. The last one brought in Joni James, flashing a three-carat diamond. Her promised was along, and they're to be married in early December. The other day going into Los Angeles (it was 95 degrees there for Nov. 9, a record), we carried the President of RKO Pictures, Bill Dozier and wife, whom I recognized as the former Ann Rutherford. Remember her? I saw my aunt and uncle and cousins in Los Angeles, and we went down to old Vera Street, a Mexican settlement and the original one in this giant city. My last trip there, I really had a big thrill, and this is how it all came about.

During a tour through Republic Studios and lunch in the commissary, I met actor Scott Brady, who was making a picture there. He is best known for his roles in Western films and television. He's one of Hollywood's most eligible bachelors — 6'3" and all that. Good looking, and he has a rugged appeal. Well, I got to meet him, and we fell to talking, and he asked me for a date that night, which I (of course!) accepted. We had a most enjoyable evening. He's quite nice, and I'll have to tell you about it sometime. And I still haven't quite gotten over it — my date with a movie star, though after all, I keep telling myself, they're just people, too, so why the big fuss? Nevertheless...

Tonight, we head for home, and I'll probably be teaching, as I have been, almost every day. What with company and dates and such full days, no wonder my "to answer" mail piles up. No doubt you have the same problem. The 18th, I leave on an Olympic charter south to Melbourne and Sydney that should be interesting, and when I get home again, it will be December 2nd, then 1957!

I haven't been accomplishing too much book readings the last two or so months. I used to average one a trip, but now I consider myself lucky to wade through one month's magazines before the next one comes out. I saw some good movies lately: Bad Seed, Tea and Sympathy, Eddie Duchin Story, Somebody Up There Likes Me, and Solid Gold Cadillac. I'm looking forward now to Giant and War and Peace. I saw Judith Anderson last month in San Francisco in The Chalk Garden. She's great! Also chalked up two more plays — Damn Yankees and Anniversary Waltz. I'm suffering from writer's cramps at this point, as my increasingly poor script testifies. It's been great, Carol, having this little chat with you again; one-sided though it may have been, it's the best we can do. Bye for now.

Love and keep me posted, Marie

# Chapter 25

## Hotel Rex, Sidney, Australia
### March 23, 1957

Dear Carol,

This letter is being sent to you from the Fijis, an island country with 333 islands in the South Pacific Ocean. I've been carrying around your long, newsy letter dated January, I'm ashamed to admit. But anyway, now that I've succeeded in arriving at this point, I should really set the stage. If you were here now, I think you would be reminded of one of those summers at camp – there's that something in the air – warm sunny days, a blue haze on the mountains, lush verdant tropicana everywhere, sporting facilities (I just came from a session of tennis and a combination swim-sunbath), and our meals, served by the natives, are taken in the crew quarters' mess hall. In the evenings, we have movies, old but good; tonight, it's *The Lost Weekend*, and that took an Academy Award in the late '40s, I'm sure. This is also where I catch up on my reading and letter-writing.

We're on our way home now from Sidney, and I will arrive Wednesday in time for the Academy Award presentations on TV that night. I always look forward to them. This makes four years in a row that I will have been in for them. I am missing Monday night, though – "One Minute to Ditch" on the

Robert Montgomery show, the story of the Pan Am crash landing in the Pacific last October. I would so love to be reconciled. This is an English typewriter that I'm using here (this is a British colony), and several of the keys are rearranged from our system, so you must excuse my pound signs that might crop up.

We're also a day ahead of you, having crossed the International Date Line, so back home where you are, it's only Friday. I hope your exam marks and term papers came back with the kind of decoration that would please you. And if not doing a thesis but taking another semester instead is what permits your being there in July, then I'm glad you made that decision. I just heard yesterday, however, that the company has cancelled all flight service vacations for May — guess we've been awarded several military charters we didn't expect — so here's hoping everything is squared away by the end of June. This much I know: we must receive a full month's notice of any change, which means that if Memorial Day passes with no word, all will go as planned. And, Carol, you can believe this or not, but I'm looking forward to that little stay with you in Gainesville more than any other phase of this much anticipated whirl.

Remember outlining my proposed itinerary to you at Christmastime, so won't go into that again. Can let you know my exact (though tentative) schedule by early June. I will be arriving from Miami by Eastern, and the flight I prefer arrives in Gainesville in the morning about 9:30, unless there's a change. I'm so looking ahead to our sharing that 4-poster! How many years has it been since 160 Sly Avenue, anyway? Remember those oatmeal cookies, the hard-boiled eggs, tuna sandwiches, and the muffins that Joyce brought down that we used to supplement our budget? What fun! We'll have a bang-up time of it, I'm sure. But this much I want to say, and that's I know you'll be in school, and I don't want or expect you to disrupt the pattern of that new scholastic life, so don't feel you have to make any plans for me. I'll enjoy just wandering around the campus, investigating and exploring, while you're busy. Oh, to be in an academic setting once again! But I'll bet it's all quite different from Keuka. That possible side-trip to St. Augustine sounds particularly fun.

Dot will be arriving stateside any day now. I heard from Mother, who heard from Mrs. Lawson, that Joyce had received a note from Dot asking her to reserve a certain weekend in April for their reunion. Oh, that the four of us could be there together again! About the new address – it's Apt. 2, 1445 Bellevue, Burlingame, California, and the best setup yet. My new roommate is my only one now, a welcome change from living with a minimum of four since college days, and she isn't airline but a nurse in the San Mateo schools. A bit older than I, she comes from Tacoma and is the sweetest, most considerate person you could hope to find. Unfortunately, she is thinking of taking an overseas job with the state department after this school term, but so far nothing definite. The place itself is a dream, furnished in grand style, and with a follow-through color scheme of gray. We even have a large screen TV set that can be viewed from either the divan or our beds at night. Out back by the patio, a happy little brook gurgles along (isn't that poetic?); we each have carports; the "price is right"; and it's centrally located, yet in a nice residential part of town, the library being just half a block away!

Wish you could come visit me! Think that might be arranged? Ellen and I have fun, too, taking turns getting dinner. I've tried out scads of new recipes lately that I'd cut out of magazines over the years and been meaning to try. Joyce wrote me about your visit at Christmas time, how they all enjoyed having you and all that you did. Yes, I was well looked after myself this year. I arrived home from a grand Tokyo trip the 22nd, and on Monday, Christmas Eve Day, early, I drove south to San Fernando and had a pleasant holiday stay with the Los Angeles clan of the McGraths. I talked to the folks back home and just all in all had a grand time. The temperature was in the 70's all week. Yes, Thursday Scott Brady called and invited me out for dinner. It was about 3:35, and I was preparing dinner for the evening, as Ruth was away for the day. So, what did I *do but invite him over. He accepted, and we all spent a nice family-type night of it, with the Christmas tree lights beaming and Kenneth's toys (my nephew) all around. We watched the fights on TV, of all things, and after the others had discreetly retired, we just talked and talked into the wee hours. A pleasant relief to be with someone in a line other than airplanes. And he brought me what I'd swear is a half-gallon of Arpege cologne. Wasn't that sweet? That's probably the end of that, but yes, haven't I been rich in experiences of meeting people, going places, and seeing things? Don't think I don't keep reminding myself of it.*

*Shortly after the first of the year, I had a publicity stunt to appear on Barry Sullivan's TV show, The Man Called X, in a scene in which Pan Am figured. I only appeared on the screen about 15 or so seconds, but we had a lot of fun, got to meet the star, were paid by the shooting company, and received flight time to the song of four hours from Pan Am, too. I was surprised to hear you were an Ike booster this past election. You know you were one of the staunchest Kefauver-Stevenson-Democratic ticket boosters our junior year during those demonstrations. How could the rest of us forget? So, clue me in — what happened? Anyway, welcome to the winning side. These certainly are prosperous times we're living in, aren't they? I just hope things continue along as they are.*

*When in Gainesville, I will be anxious to see Kim*[023] *and your father, too. After looking at that picture on your dresser all through college, I feel that I already know him well. And speaking of my brothers...after Bob's graduation last June, he worked for three or so months for Alcoa on that St. Lawrence Waterway Project, then, in November, he went into the service. He was stationed in Virginia, and now he is home having completed his training. He is a Second Lieutenant! He ships out from the west coast for the Far East in April, and he will be in Oakland for a few days before that. So, in two weeks, we're looking forward to having a couple of days together when I can show him the sights of San Francisco.*

---

023      My brother

*Haven't there been some excellent movies filmed this past year? Don't miss Around the World in 80 Days. It's terrific! And reading Giant only heightened my enjoyment of that movie. Didn't you love that? I just saw Teahouse the week before I flew this trip. I had seen the play in London with John Forsythe, and I must admit that this is one adaptation that wasn't in the least bit spoiled in the process; in fact, I thought that it was even funnier as a movie. Then, there was Anastasia and War and Peace, but these two slightly disappointed me; their buildups were so great. Ten Commandments is next on my list, and there have been ever so many more.*

*You asked about any further trips. If I'm in over the Easter vacation, since school will be closed then, I hope to take an excursion by Volkswagen to Lake Tahoe, which everyone says is so lovely. Then, skirt the few miles to Carson City, Virginia City, and Reno, doubling back down to spend a couple of days at Yosemite. Here, it is almost Easter already! What do you know – it'll be July before we know it. I hope to hear from you before then, and I'll let you know as soon as I do about our coming reunion. Whoop-de-doo!*

*Love, Marie*

On June 17, 1957, Marie sent me a congratulation card commemorating my antici-pated graduation from the University of Florida in August with my master's degree. On it, she wrote:

*I'm back from vacation and in route now to Tokyo, Hong Kong, and Bangkok, the capital of Thailand. Congratulations, "Master!" Drop a line when you're settled and let's hear the scoop on your new adventure.*

*Love, Marie*

# Chapter 26

## Gainesville, Florida
### July 6, 1957

Dear Carol,

I had a wonderful several days with you in Gainesville, Florida. I'm so proud of you graduating in August with your master's degree. I enjoyed sitting on the back seat of your dad's Italian Lambretta as you drove us around the campus. It was fun catching up on all our activities and meeting your professor dad and brother. I thought you'd like to hear how I fared travelling back to "Yankee Land." Well, thought I was really in for it at the Jacksonville airport. When I first checked in, they said space available on the 4:25 p.m. flight was questionable. If I didn't make it, I would have a layover for a full day, as all succeeding flights were full. It was 95 degrees in Jax, and I didn't relish the prospect, so I breathed easy when the plane finally took off at 5 p.m. with me on board. My flight to Syracuse from Charlotte was due to leave at 8:40 p.m., and we didn't even land until 9 p.m., but wonders of wonders, that flight was late, too. I didn't have a reservation either, but because I was alone and due to other "fortuitous circumstances," I made it all right.

So, here I'm at home and my feet are almost completely healed. It's almost high noon, and I was reminiscing about last week in Gainesville. Just a bit ago, remember, we were picnicking. I had such a pleasant stay with you. You are one top notch hostess and guide. I'd heartedly recommend you to any prospective guest. The weather here in Auburn has been ideal so far — cool breezy days of sunshine registering in the high 70's usually.

I haven't seen Joyce yet, but this morning I received a letter from Phyllis. She's met Warren's family, and this relationship seems destined for the altar. She took her vacation in early June and the two of them were in Philadelphia for a wedding. They called on Lili and baby. So, I enjoyed the Alumnae News. Say hello to Marge, Joanne, and Mrs. K[024], your dad and Kim, too. The shoes I left at your house arrived in fine shape. Many thanks. Drop me a line when you're settled in Tallahassee, and let's hear the scoop on your new adventure. Bye for now.

Love, Marie

024    My three housemates in Gainesville

# Chapter 27

## Tallahassee, Florida
### August 26, 1957

Dear Carol,

I mailed you a card for your August birthday. It had a picture of fall leaves and a beautiful scenery which made me sort of homesick for home. If these were still our Keuka days, we'd be packing up about now for a new semester. It was always a few days after your birthday and though this is the actual date, I hope by the time it reaches your new address, you'll be there, too. Your card from the Sunshine Skyway was here to greet me when I returned from a trip (a personal one, this time), and before that I was most proud to find your name under the Guidance section of your graduation program. We'll be anxious now to hear all the details of your grades, trip, new job, locale, and situation there – also news of your mother's sojourn in Paris. That was a surprise, and I am so glad she could make it to the Sorbonne. How are your housemates, Marge, Joanne, and Mrs. Kirkpatrick? Just this morning, I brought in the roll of film to be developed, which contains those shots from my vacation. I'm anxious to see how they turned out.

Did I tell you that one day while home, Joyce and I drove over to Geneva, then to Newark. It was a grand day of shopping and visiting Jo Bates and Betsy

Atwater. Both have such handsome families and seem so content. I've been back in San Mateo exactly a month now, arriving back from another ferry flight the 26th. On the third, I left on a two-week Tokyo-Hong Kong-Bangkok trip that was a good one.

I don't leave again until September 9th and that will be to London on our inaugural polar route. There should be lots of fanfare and fun, and I'm so excited about going to Europe again. You'd think it was my very first trip. I just returned yesterday from a Sunday "sleeping bag" motor excursion with a friend to upper California and Oregon. Crater Lake is indescribably breathtaking. That, along with seeing the Ice Follies and the musical Fanny is about all the news here.

Many happy returns and lots of love, Marie

# Chapter 28

## *Romance of the Skies*
### *November 8, 1957*

Marie wasn't scheduled to take another flight, as she was on a week's respite. However, when she received a phone call from another stewardess, who wasn't feeling well, she offered to take her place on the Clipper *Romance of the Skies*.

On November 8, 1957, this Pan America Stratocruiser crashed into the Pacific Ocean at the Point of No Return.

**The Associated Press wrote:**

### AUBURN GIRL STEWARDESS

*"We're just hoping and praying now. That's all there is to do," Mrs. Robert E. McGrath said Saturday from her home at 60 Capitol Street.*

*The couple's only daughter, pretty 26-year-old Marie, a Pan American Airways stewardess, was missing on a San Francisco to Hawaii flight. Marie, a graduate of St. Alphonsus School, East High, and Keuka College, is a substitute teacher in Burlingame and San Mateo County, California, between flights. She was last home on a July vacation.*

*"She was in all kinds of activities," Mrs. McGrath said. "Marie was on the dean's list and editor of the college literary magazine. She loved sports."*

*McGrath is a superintendent at New York State Electric and Gas Corporation.*

## A newspaper from Honolulu, reported on November 9:

A Coast Guard cutter sped today toward two bobbing yellow objects, possibly life rafts, near the spot more than 1,000 miles east of Honolulu where a Pan American Stratocruiser disappeared last night with 44 people aboard.

An Air Force plane, part of a massive sea-air search group, sighted the cylindrical objects in the Pacific Ocean. They were 80 miles southwest of the last position reported by the Honolulu-bound transport, Romance of the Skies. That routine last word came at 5:40 p.m. yesterday.

However, the Navy said the object may be disposable jet fuel tanks. The Coast Guard commander directing the search said there was a "potent possibility" the plane "suddenly and for an unknown reason went out of control." The four-engine plane, after passing the Point of No Return halfway along the 2,400-mile flight from San Francisco, mysteriously vanished without reporting any trouble once. The transport's fuel supply is estimated to have given out at 3 a.m.

The Coast Guard cutter Minnetonka was part of a search party of more than 29 planes and 14 surface vessels covering charted miles. Cmdr. William E. Chapline, heading the Coast Guard phase of the search, grimly pointed out that the ditched plane should have been able to flash some distress signal during a 20-minute descent from 10,000 feet. Failing that, there should be signals from hand-cranked radio transmitters on life crafts – if any were launched. The weather offered no obstacle to the missing plane.

Among the 36 passengers were a State Department official, a chemical company executive, and a French air ace of World War II. They were bound for Honolulu, Tokyo, Hong Kong, or Rangoon. There was not even a hint of trouble when the plane's captain, Gordon H. Brown, radioed last night at 5:04 p.m. that his position was 1,028 miles east of Honolulu. After that – awesome silence.

Chapline noted that the plane was well-built and might float indefinitely after being ditched. There were no frontal storms reported along the plane's flight path. The transport had run into headwinds, but they were not strong.

**A News Gram by Radio WMEN, dated November 15, 1957:**

*Passengers aboard ill-fated Pan American Airliner apparently had ample warning before the crash. A Navy expert said 17 bodies found showed passengers had time to don life jackets before the crash.*

For years, the crash remained unsolved. It was considered one of the worst aviation disasters in American history. There were many theories as to what happened to the plane. Was it sabotaged by a crew member, bombed by a deranged passenger, or did one of the passengers buy a life insurance policy that would go to the beneficiary that might have caused the crash?

It had been a mystery over the years. The reason for the crash haunted Gregg Herken and Ken Fortenberry for many years. Ken's father was the navigator, and Gregg's favorite elementary school teacher, Marie McGrath, was the stewardess on this plane. They both authored an article in the Air and Space magazine in January 2017, entitled, "What Happened to Pan Am Flight 7?" They believe they have found the answer to the cause of the crash which they researched for 13 years.

The discovery of the transcript of 944's mayday call and the cowl ring fragment point to the conclusion that *Romance of the Skies* had crashed because of a catastrophic mechanical failure, not a bomb. Gregg Herken, who wrote in the above article what might have caused the crash, was an elementary student in a San Mateo, California school where Marie taught as a substitute teacher when she was free from her flights. He said, "When our regular teacher went on maternity leave, our class came to know and love Miss McGrath, who one day held a 'luau' for us kids. We were all secretly sad when our regular teacher returned to work and Marie went back to flying."

Persons interested in reading more about *Romance of the Skies* can go to the Internet: https://www.ucmeced.edu/content/gregg-herken.com.

# Epilogue

At 26 years old and about four years as a stewardess, Marie Louise McGrath fulfilled her lifelong goal of flying high in the sky overseas on a Pan American World Airlines Stratocruiser—something she had dreamed about all through her college years. She loved her experiences with Pan Am. She had so much fun traveling all over Europe and the Far East, but she never saw all she wanted to see. She loved meeting so many famous people.

Many years later, we learned of an engagement from Brian Casidy, the husband of Dottie Wingert Casidy, who was on a Pan Am flight from Japan. He was dumbfounded when he learned that the pilot with whom he was sitting had been engaged to Marie. None of her friends ever knew this, although Marie was not silent about her love affairs.

Marie never attained retirement from the airlines to pursue another dream—to become an entrepreneur of an antique shop in Auburn, New York, or become a wife and mother.

Marie's parents were kept in constant touch of any information about her survival. Throughout the search, Pan American World Airlines had them hooked up to a communication system so that they could stay in touch with the search.

Marie's body was never recovered. The sad part of this crash—Marie wasn't scheduled to take this flight. She replaced another stewardess who was sick. Although stewardesses are now called flight attendants, I chose to use the title that Marie was given to her at the time of her employment.

Ken Fortenberry and Gregg Herken formed the Flight 7 Memorial Committee to honor the victims of the crash. In 2023, they dedicated a memorial on the grounds of Millbrae City Hall.

The Clipper *Romance of the Skies* was a Boeing 377 Stratocruiser that is no longer in use today. At one time, it was the largest commercial airliner by passenger volume and miles flown worldwide for decades as recorded by the Pan American Museum Foundation, which has an exhibit about this plane with pictures and memorabilia located in the Cradle of Aviation Museum, Garden City, New York. This plane was decommissioned in 1961, but its legacy as a luxury plane lives on.

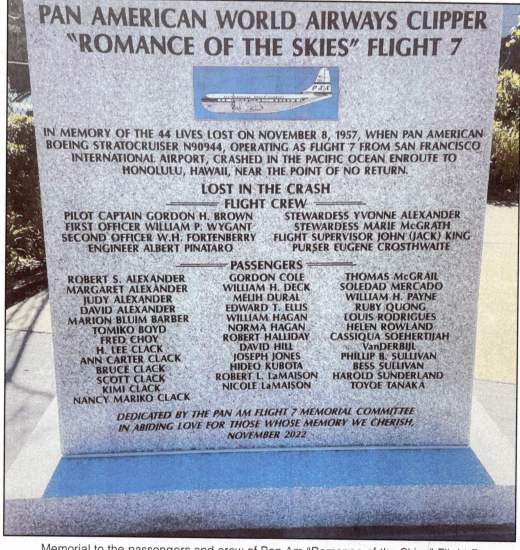

Memorial to the passengers and crew of Pan Am "Romance of the Skies" Flight 7 at the Millbrae History Museum near San Francisco International Airport.

# Resources

Cradle of Aviation Museum, Garden City, NY.

Gregg Herken and Ken Fortenberry, "The Mystery of the Lost Clipper," *Air and Space Magazine*, September 2004.

Photograph of "Romance in the Sky" submitted by Ken H. Fortenberry.

Ken H. Fortenberry, *Flight 7 is Missing*, Fayetteville Mafia Press, Columbus, Ohio.

Letters written by Marie McGrath to Carol Ann Patterson.

*Miami Herald*, Miami, Florida, November 10, 1957.

News Gram by Radio WMEN, November 15, 1957.

*Tallahassee Democrat*, Tallahassee, Florida, November 7, 1957.

*The Citizen-Advertiser*, Auburn, NY, February 10, 1954.

The Pan American Museum Foundation.

Photograph of a Pan American Airways Boeing 377 Stratocruiser submitted by Terry Morgan.

# Acknowledgments

I am honored to have Dr. Gregg Herken, Professor History Emeritus, University of California at Merced, California, write the Foreword and provide the memorial picture honoring the persons who lost their lives on the *Romance of the Skies*. I am grateful to Ken H. Fortenberry, who provided me with the picture of Pan Am N90944, *Romance of the Skies*, a plane similar to the one on which Marie McGrath was the stewardess and Ken's father was the navigator.

I also appreciated my friend, Marilyn Butler, and my son, Scott Patterson Boyles, who critiqued my manuscript, offering valuable suggestions for additional information. Scott also provided his expertise in computer technology, which assisted me greatly.

I am most appreciative of the excellent graphics prepared by Graphic Designer, Tara Sizemore, and the support of the publisher, Janie C. Jessee.

It has been a joy to write this book, reliving so many memories. Marie was a special friend, and I miss her.

# About the Author

Carol Ann Patterson Boyles-Jernigan's professional career encompassed 50 years as an administrator at Keuka College, Florida State University, Central Florida Community College (now College of Central Florida), and retirement from the University of North Florida. She received her BA from Keuka College, the M.Ed., and advanced courses from the University of Florida. Her accomplishments are listed in *Who's Who In America* and *Who's Who in the World*.

She is a member of DAR, the Association of University Women (AAUW), and the Winthrop Society. Mrs. Boyles-Jernigan is the author of *The Safety Deposit Shock: Your Secrets Will Find You Out* and *Around the Next Bend: An Adventure In Borneo*. She lives in Blountville, Tenn., and may be contacted at molly7804@aol.com.

Printed in the USA
CPSIA information can be obtained
at www.ICGtesting.com
CBHW042033121124
17314CB00034B/1084